Geophilosophy of the Mediterranean

SUNY series in Contemporary Italian Philosophy
———————
Silvia Benso and Brian Schroeder, editors

Geophilosophy of the Mediterranean

Caterina Resta

Edited by
Rita Fulco, Sandro Gorgone,
Giuliana Gregorio, and Valentina Surace

Translated by
Aisling Reid and Valentina Surace

Published by State University of New York Press, Albany

© 2012 Mesogea by Sabir s.r.l., Messina, Italy

Translation © 2024 State University of New York

All rights reserved

Printed in the United States of America

No part of this book may be used or reproduced in any manner whatsoever without written permission. No part of this book may be stored in a retrieval system or transmitted in any form or by any means including electronic, electrostatic, magnetic tape, mechanical, photocopying, recording, or otherwise without the prior permission in writing of the publisher.

For information, contact State University of New York Press, Albany, NY
www.sunypress.edu

Library of Congress Cataloging-in-Publication Data

Names: Resta, Caterina, author | Fulco, Rita, 1972– editor. | Gorgone,
Sandro, editor. | Gregorio, Giuliana, editor. | Surace, Valentina,
editor, translator. | Reid, Aisling, translator.
Title: Geophilosophy of the Mediterranean / Caterina Resta ; edited by Rita
Fulco, Sandro Gorgone, Giuliana Gregorio, and Valentina Surace ;
translated by Aisling Reid and Velentina Surace.
Other titles: Geofilosofia del Mediterraneo. English
Description: Description: Albany, NY : State University of New York Press,
[2024]. | Series: SUNY series in contemporary Italian philosophy |
Includes bibliographical references and index.
Identifiers: LCCN 2023039272 | ISBN 9781438497594 (hardcover : alk.
paper) | ISBN 9781438497600 (ebook) | ISBN 9781438497587 (pbk. :
alk. paper)
Subjects: LCSH: Mediterranean Region—Geography. | Mediterranean
Region—Civilization—Philosophy.
Classification: LCC D973 .R43713 2024 | DDC 910.9182/2—dc23/eng/20240126
LC record available at https://lccn.loc.gov/2023039272

To Gianvito Resta,
Scholar of Mediterranean Sicily

Contents

List of Illustrations	ix
Acknowledgments	xi
Editors' Note	xiii
Preface *Caterina Resta*	xvii
1. Atlantics or Mediterraneans?	1
2. Europe to Come	13
3. A Sea That Unites and Divides	35
4. Cartographies of Italy	51
5. The Origin of Messina	67
Notes	81
Index	101
About the Author	103

Illustrations

Figure 4.1	The Northern League's upside-down Italy.	52
Figure 4.2	Ebstorf *Mappa mundi*.	55
Figure 4.3	Al-Idrisi's circular world map.	58
Figure 4.4	Al-Idrisi's *Tabula Rogeriana* with detail showing the Mediterranean.	59
Figure 4.5	Al-Idrisi's *Gulf of Naples and Islands*.	61
Figure 4.6	Al-Idrisi's *Sicily*.	61
Figure 5.1	Miniature of the city of Messina, artist unknown.	67

Acknowledgments

The idea for this translation arose from an important event that is a pivotal milestone for the editors: Professor Caterina Resta's retirement. Each of us has had a unique and profound relationship with Resta, who served as a scholarly mentor and a personal guide.

This volume is as a heartfelt expression of gratitude toward Resta. We deeply appreciate the time, wisdom, and attentive support she consistently provided to us. Nor are we the only beneficiaries of her generous attention; countless young students and scholars have also been fortunate to experience Resta's exceptional teaching. This edition is, therefore, a tribute to all that she selflessly offered throughout her academic career.

We extend a special thanks to those who contributed to the translation, particularly Aisling Reid, a lecturer at Queen's University Belfast who has admired Caterina Resta's work for many years.

Our gratitude also extends to Silvia Benso, who, from the very beginning, has enthusiastically welcomed the project into the esteemed SUNY series in Contemporary Italian Philosophy, which she codirects with Brian Schroeder. Benso has long been dedicated to promoting Italian thought, with a special emphasis on women's contributions. Our collaboration with Benso and the Society for Italian Philosophy (SIP) has been important and fruitful, resulting in both academic dialogue and genuine friendship.

We would also like to extend our warmest thanks to Brian Schroeder, the coeditor of the series, and to Michael Rinella, who meticulously oversaw the editorial process for this volume with professionalism, care, and patience.

Editors' Note

The term *geophilosophy* probably took on a theoretically important meaning for the first time in the title of chapter 4 of Gilles Deleuze and Félix Guattari's book *Qu'est-ce que la philosophie?*[1] Although pointing out this first use, in her *Intervista sulla Geofilosofia*, Caterina Resta emphasizes how in that case the term remained within the perspective of the two philosophers and distant from her own.[2]

The term became especially popular among French theorists after the 1993 publication of the collected volume *Penser l'Europe à ses frontières*, whose heading was "Géophilosophie de l'Europe." It is in Italy, however, that the term has become most philosophically salient thanks to two important volumes by Massimo Cacciari, *Geofilosofia dell'Europa* and *L'Arcipelago*.[3] It was these two volumes that most inspired Resta's thought; she describes them as "an inescapable diptych for anyone wishing to approach a geophilosophical perspective, from both a theoretical and a philosophical-political point of view."[4]

Resta's thought is, in fact, entirely geophilosophical. It is no coincidence that her first volume on Heidegger, *La misura della differenza: Saggi su Heidegger*,[5] focuses at length on geophilosophical concepts such as "measure," or *Heimkunft* (that is, the return home), as well as on the relationship between Heaven and Earth as it relates to the Heideggerian concept of *Geviert*. Resta's geophilosophical perspective is particularly apparent in the subsequent volumes she dedicated to Heidegger: *Il luogo e le vie: Geografie del pensiero in Martin Heidegger* and *La terra del mattino: Ethos, Logos e Physis nel*

xiii

xiv EDITORS' NOTE

pensiero di Martin Heidegger.[6] Both works explore important geophilosophical concepts like "place," "border," "limit," and "earth."

Resta's philosophy was also deeply influenced by Carl Schmitt's geopolitics, as is apparent in her stimulating publication *Stato mondiale o* Nomos *della terra: Carl Schmitt tra universo e pluriverso*, where she refers in particular to the binomial Earth and Sea that Schmitt used as key to interpreting universal history.[7]

But only her scholarly interest in authors like Emmanuel Levinas, Jacques Derrida, and Jean-Luc Nancy have enabled Resta to clearly outline the idea of a "geophilosophy of hospitality," which she proposes as a framework to rethink the ways in which the human being "dwells" on the earth. In this regard, the following publications by Resta are of particular note: *L'evento dell'altro: Etica e politica in Jacques Derrida, L'Estraneo: Ostilità e ospitalità nel pensiero del Novecento*, and *La passione dell'impossibile: Saggi su Jacques Derrida.*[8]

The present volume on the geophilosophy of the Mediterranean, which was published in Italy in 2012, should be contextualized within the broader scope of Resta's thinking as one of her lines of research but also as a perspective that pervades and gives a specific character to her entire reflection.

For Resta, the Mediterranean is not only a place of incomparable beauty and variety of cultures but "the model par excellence of what should be understood as culture: a geohistorical space in which different civilizations, clashing and/or meeting, fighting and/or dialoguing, have transformed these multiplicities not into a flat monoculture but into a plural identity composed of differences that, despite a thousand difficulties, tend to be reflected in a single sea, revealing unmistakable common traits."[9] She considers the plural identity that typifies the Mediterranean as an antidote to any myth of autochthony and identity closure without renouncing identity or indulging in the indistinct mixing of heterogeneous elements that characterizes certain forms of multiculturalism.

This is why we believe that, at a historical juncture in which wars are gaining ground and claiming victims, the English translation of this volume can be an important contribution to the

EDITORS' NOTE

exercise of a critical thinking capable of grasping the potential of the geophilosophical perspective. To quote Resta, "if culture is always the cultivation of what belongs more properly to specific traditions and to a specific history, nevertheless, precisely for this reason, it can only keep itself alive to the extent that it remains open to confrontation with other cultures, allowing itself to be crossed by what is not 'proper' to it."[10]

Rita Fulco, Sandro Gorgone,
Giuliana Gregorio, Valentina Surace
Messina, 15 April 2023

Preface

Caterina Resta

For a long time, I have lived with the Mediterranean never crossing my mind, and I have made many plans to escape. When I was young, like many others, I dreamed of escaping, of moving away from a land that seemed inhospitable to me, resistant to cultural change, devoid of stimuli, on the margins of history, condemned to underdevelopment, backwardness, narrow-mindedness, ignorance, cronyism, and the Mafia. I spent the years of my postgraduate training "outside"—far from the Island of Sicily, away from its claustrophobic closure. Paris, Pavia, Milan, and Rome were the stations dotted along a tortuous escape route. I had no clear sense of where I wanted to land, as long as it was far from whence I had come. I did not even have deep roots in the place I was leaving; I came from a family who had moved to Messina from another place. Therefore, I did not even notice that I was losing that slender attachment to the place, which had matured during my childhood, until every weak bond was severed and every fragile root had dried up. Uprooting and strangeness became my norm, my wound, and an unexpected opportunity for me. I crossed time and space with no fixed abode and no long-term plans. My only compass was my voracious, insatiable intellectual curiosity, whose bites I now regret. During that formative journey far from my native land—which was, for many young Europeans of the time, a must, and whose necessity today I, too, understand—I collated at random

xviii   PREFACE

an archive of experiences that would last me for the rest of my life, and I now see them as a most precious and fruitful inheritance. Those restless, rambling, but fruitful years of apprenticeship, which were destined to germinate in the future, were spent wandering and letting myself be affected by what I encountered. The German word *Erfahrung* relates to the profound meaning of experience, understood as an itinerary full of encounters that transform us, to the extent that we are ready to embrace them. Likewise, this was the educational aim of the "grand tour" as described by the great travelers of the past, who were attracted by the sunny charm of the Mediterranean shores.

I must confess that it was only the demands of work that led me, in spite of myself, to retrace my steps and return to the Island and the city that I thought I had abandoned once and for all. My return was certainly not a coincidence, in retrospect. Rather, it was the destined need to follow, in my wanderings, at least one North Star: my desire to continue studying, my passion for research. But by then I had become foreign to the land that had generated me. For a long time, the certainty I felt of a long-term imprisonment seemed my life sentence. Frequently, I would attempt to escape and would find myself summarily returned back into my prison. Messina was—and, in some ways, continues to be—my penitentiary. I saw nothing around me but the walls of my cell, in which, like the medieval monks, I devoted myself in solitary practice to my studies. It would take too long to describe—and I can only do it retrospectively—the slow and tiring approach to what was so close to my eyes as to remain stubbornly invisible. Some unexpected physical and mental journeys, under the guidance of other people with trained eyes, finally allowed me to *see*. It was a matter, above all, of a series of trips around the Island in search of pristine beaches or necropolises, baroque churches or disused sulfur mines, ancient ruins or rural landscapes, small villages or desolate moors. I am endlessly grateful to all those who snatched me, sometimes almost with violence, from my sedentary lifestyle and my prejudices, to force me to look *outside*, teaching me the difficult art of seeing my land. If today I can say that the veil of forgetfulness which

PREFACE xix

has long covered my eyes is slowly beginning to tear, I owe it to Nicola Aricò, who somehow forced me to reflect on my hometown for the first time, on its forgotten Mediterranean origins, between the Sickle (Falce) and Peloro. I am grateful to Maria Minicuci, who accompanied me on numerous and adventurous forays on the Island. Her gaze, as an ethnologist of Mediterranean cultures, was like a lighthouse that illuminated for me unimaginable horizons for the first time. But my reconciliation, or rather my "recognition" and "gratitude" toward Sicily and the Mediterranean—a journey that is far from over—also owes a great deal to Luisa Bonesio for her great passion for archaeology and her ability to grasp the many facets that the Sicilian landscape opens up to those who can read its unmistakable features. It is only through *another* and a stranger way of seeing, coming from the "outside," that we are able to truly grasp the sense of a place that we believe to be "ours."

In this way, having become alien to myself and helped along by the eyes of others, I was able to *return* to the place of my origins and finally feel it as my deepest root. It allowed me to be able to *think* it.

This would not have been possible without the discovery of a *different way of thinking*. Geophilosophy[1] represented, for me, the possibility of bringing thought back to questioning the overall meaning of human dwelling on earth. Faced with the growing standardization of the global world, which effaces all differences and singularities, uprooting and destroying cultural identities everywhere, geophilosophy intends, rather, to grasp and safeguard the irreducible spiritual, cultural, and historical physiognomies and landscapes of communities and places. It recognizes that the meaning of our "earthly" existence can only be found in the plurality of human gatherings that inhabit times and places, each time uniquely, giving them an absolute singular and unmistakable character. They dwell in geohistorical and geosymbolic spaces that are never closed in on themselves but are instead always exposed to the coming of the other, which is the only one who is able to guarantee their life not as survival but as a flow of history that combines memory and change. Cultures that are intransitively closed within their own reassuring and alleged identities are in fact doomed to the stiffening that precedes death. It is only by incessant confrontation with otherness, with whatever or whomever comes from outside, that cultures can remain truly alive and vital. What place better exemplifies this rule than Sicily and the Mediterranean?

I began to understand that what previously had seemed to me a life sentence was in fact a privilege, in some respects. I could not, therefore, miss the opportunity to take advantage of my geo-existential location on this Island; I felt a growing need for a more conscious "dwelling" in it, primarily from a geophilosophical point of view. I had to try to *think* about the place in which roots and uprooting are constantly in conflict with one another. There is an invisible harmony that holds these opposites together. Between land and sea, this Mediterranean island has always experienced it.

In this book, I have compiled some essays that I have written and published in various locations and circumstances. They relate to this "ordeal" that has permeated my existential and philosophical research—how can they possibly be separated? I hope that the reader will be able to get a clear sense of the unitary idea that has guided their composition. They are ordered chronologically according to their publication dates, which happen, as if by magic, to coincide with the successive stages of my investigative trail. The last essay, which is dedicated to my hometown, Messina, is an exception. It was the first to be written and it was from this very text that my recollection of the forgotten Mediterranean began. I have placed it at the end because it is the signpost that the final stage of the journey has been reached, where the beginning and end meet. This long voyage through the Mediterranean lasted ten years, and I hope it will continue to get to know other ports and piers.

In the meantime, another piece of this mosaic—the unveiling of the Island and the Mediterranean—has found its place in my eyes. After spending over a year sorting my father's books after his death in order to give them a new home, I understand for the first time how tirelessly he researched Sicilian culture, even though Sicily was only an adopted homeland to him. I dedicate this book to him. He will not be able to read it, but I hope it repays a tiny

PREFACE

xxi

part of what I owe to him. It is only now, day after day among his papers, that I am slowly and painfully beginning to acknowledge, with infinite gratitude, the debt I owe to him.

Finally, I owe a special thanks to Ugo Magno and Caterina Pastura, who have long urged me to publish this collection of essays and include it in the prestigious La Piccola series of Mesogea Press. Today, I understand more clearly the destination of that long journey that began in our university years and that we have each pursued with our own methods and via our own routes, yet *together*. It was a journey by sea, a long crossing, full of stops, delays, and bewilderment, as is always the case when "coasting" the Mediterranean. It is only at the end of it that I finally found the landing place. On reaching my destination, I found them patiently waiting for my arrival.

One

Atlantics or Mediterraneans?

A Stormy Sea

What seas are our fast boats cutting through? What winds swell their unfurled sails? In which sea are we sailing? Between long-standing endemic conflicts, new revolts, and the usual crossing of migrants driven by despair, the waters of the Mediterranean are tinged with red—an ancient color, like the purple of the Phoenicians. The Mediterranean: it is a sea that has always been on fire but has also always been able to extinguish its fires and transform clashes into encounters, to change the warfront into a fruitful confrontation, *pólemos* (war) into *diálogos* (dialogue). When things have been most tense, this sea has been able to glimpse the invisible and the most powerful harmony that lies at the bottom of every dispute and restrains adversaries.[1] Sooner or later, will this sea become aware of its own size? Will it find the equilibrium between land and sea that is inscribed in its name? But Mediterranean winds of war blow ever farther, passing through and over the Balkans, until they reach remote lands that are almost forgotten by history. It is impossible not to see that one war births another; after the fall of the Twin Towers, one war means the outbreak of another, even the revelation of its very truth. As Mediterraneans, we had perhaps deluded ourselves into thinking that we could treat the Arab-Israeli conflict as a "modern" war—that is to say, as a land

1

war that stemmed from issues regarding borders, frontiers, and lands to be conquered. Even though the frequent terrorist attacks suggested that it was increasingly difficult to contain this war, it nevertheless appeared to us as limited, curable, and governable, and peace seemed close at hand. But the radicalization of the conflict revealed to us the fragility of our illusions and of any attempts to "reshape" a war in the era of globalization. Since this new form of "global war" emerged,[2] we have no longer been under any illusions about our ability to contain conflicts or restrict wars within clearly delineated spatial boundaries. Behind the mask of humanitarian intervention, all recent conflicts, including the wars in Iraq, the Balkans conflict, and the war against the Taliban in Afghanistan, have revealed the radicalization of postmodern war, which has buried forever every idea of *jus publicum europaeum*, of a European public law, as well as the possibility of containing conflicts. Carl Schmitt, with extraordinary clarity and foresight, had foreseen all this. His sharp gaze retraced the stations of the *via crucis*, the way of the cross that gradually shifted the focus of world history from Europe and "its" sea (the Mediterranean) to America and the boundless oceanic expanse that surrounds it and constitutes its very being.[3] Hegel already noted that "the European state is truly European only in so far as it has links with the sea."[4] According to a recurrent literary motif,[5] Europe appeared as a small promontory, a cape, a peninsula of the great Asian continent, and the Mediterranean as an internal sea that is everywhere surrounded by land. On the other side, America, when compared with old Europe, is a New World. Hegel saw it as "the country of the future, whose world-historical importance has yet to be revealed in the ages which lie ahead—perhaps in a conflict between North and South."[6] As a large island in comparison to the small island of England that gave birth to it, America does not understand the limits of the *mesógeos* (midlands) sea nor those of the *póntos*, a sea that is a road and bridge over which to cross and join lands.[7] America is surrounded by an ocean, an endless stretch of water as far as the eye can see, a boundless space of Limitlessness and disproportion. America itself has been the response to the ocean's irresistible call.

On which routes did we set sail? Which cruises or crusades are we part of? Winds of war and stormy skies have often clouded the blue depth of that *mare nostrum*, our sea (as the Romans called it). Within its shining clearness, different peoples, languages, and civilizations have been mirrored from coast to coast and from one shore to the next. They certainly came into conflict with one another, but, more often, they engaged each other in dialogue and mutual understanding. Over time, they have developed shared words, such as the word *hospitality*, which crosses the entire Mediterranean, from the Greek *philoxenía*,[8] to the hospitality of Abraham[9] and of his God, who loves the foreigner,[10] to the idea inherited from Latin culture that guests must be respected.

Despite everything, Europe still faces this sea that is in continuous dialogue with the land that borders it, that holds it in check and contains it, inserting its promontories into it, indenting it with its inlets and gulfs, dotting it with islands and peninsulas. Predrag Matvejević defines it as "a sea surrounded by land or land touched by a sea."[11] Or have we perhaps embarked, without even knowing it, on a far riskier journey, beyond all limits and measures, toward the infinite, unlimited, homogeneous, and empty space of the oceanic expanse, where no land is on the horizon, neither in front of nor behind us? To which sea does Europe think it belongs? to the Mediterranean, which we still pompously refer to as the cradle of the entire Western civilization? or to that ocean that dragged Columbus past all known limits, to "discover" a New World?[12]

That "discovery" revealed, once and for all, the two souls that tear Europe apart, its constant being in *krísis* between them, and the urgent need for a decision between two shores, two worlds, two seas. Are we Atlantics? Are we Mediterraneans?

Following Ulysses's Trails

More than anyone else, Ulysses, this tireless traveler, in his double Homeric and Dantean versions, embodies this dilemma at the heart of Europe. Odysseus is a man of the Mediterranean not only because he has the features of a *polýmetis*, a crafty-minded person—his intellect is so multifaceted that it borders on deceit, to such an extent that Virgil could define him as a *scelerum inventor*, a deviser of crimes. His very journey is Mediterranean because, in it, *nóstos* and *éxodos*, homecoming and departure, continually contradict each other, like the land he must finally return to and the sea that continually seduces and tears him away. He is not a simple homeward-bound figure, as Levinas would claim, in contrast to Abraham (who is a man of departure with no return and of a land that is only a promise).[13] Rather, he is a *homo viator*, a wandering figure in continuous delay, even though he is always *oriented* toward the route home. The *Odyssey* is not only a poem about homesickness and domestic peace, nor, on the other hand, does Odysseus resemble Captain Ahab of *Moby-Dick*. His actions do not occur in the immeasurable vastness of the ocean but in the measured space of an inland sea, which is nevertheless fraught with perils.[14] Without a doubt, the prow of his ship is always directed toward home, but its keel slides lightly on the water surface, incapable of permanently docking itself. Odysseus is neither hurried nor vexed on his slow journey back from beach to beach, and each port is not only an entrance door but also an exit door, a stopover, with new departures ahead. The stopovers may be long or short; some may be more sweet and entertaining than others. Some more than others may remind him of his native land and the domestic affections that force him to return. The call that comes from the sea is just as seductive as the siren song. It makes him desire to leave, just for the sake of going. Odysseus's travel would be incomprehensible were it not for this letting himself drift away, this losing the way, the oblivion of the final destination, the continuous digressions that time and again force him to postpone the end of the journey. Between land and sea, the journey of Ulysses is truly a Mediterranean one; it is a grandiose epic of its broken coasts, peninsulas, inlets, and straits as well as its extraordinarily varied islands, from Ogygia, the island of Calypso; to Scheria, the land of the Phaeacians; to Sicily; and to Ithaca itself, to name the most famous.

The journey of Dante's Ulysses, described in canto 26 of *Inferno*, is quite different.[15] Dante's poetry, which, however ignorant Dante may have been of the Homeric *Odyssey*, nevertheless derives from Latin sources,[16] shows us a very different figure of Ulysses, one we might consider to be "Atlantic" rather than Mediterranean. Echoing Cicero and Seneca, Dante's Ulysses appears as *sapientiae cupidus*, a lover of wisdom, who is animated by *innatus cognitionis amor*, an inborn love of knowledge. He is no longer the hero who returns to his homeland, albeit delayed by countless stops; instead, he is the hero of knowledge, who pursues his companions not to stagnate but "to follow virtue and knowledge." And, in order to attain knowledge, Ulysses and his companions cannot *stay*; they must *go*. They must set sail, raise their anchors, and go beyond any limits still considered insurmountable, turning their "stern toward the morning" and leaving at the first light of day—according to some scholars—for this journey at the end of the night. Other interpreters say that they had to reverse the usual direction of their travels and point the bow to the West, "following the sun" on its declining path, traveling toward the sunset, until shipwrecked in a "mad flight."

Dante's Ulysses does not know any return journeys; he remains deaf to the call of the *oîkos*, the home where family affections, which might hold him back, await him in vain; only the passion for knowledge and a desire to *experience* the world ("the ardor that I had to / gain experience of the world") continually push him farther to "open sea." Aged amid the shores of the Mediterranean, with few companions left, he now feels its borders are too narrow and limited, as are its views. *Beyond* the Pillars of Hercules, beyond the final End that they represent for the ancient world, an end-less oceanic space opens up—the infinite sea of unconstrained knowledge. Beyond that extreme limit, he is devoured by the already-modern anxiety to try, to attempt, to test, and to finally experience the unknown. He is among the first moderns to be unable to resist the siren song of the ocean and to undergo the destructive seduction of the Limitless. The mountain of the earthly paradise will remain a "New land" that is only glimpsed, a utopian island floating on a space that is by now absolutely delocalized. It emerges and appears only for a moment, after a "nocturnal" journey into the heart of darkness, in the instant preceding the shipwreck, before the battered boat sinks into the sea with its human cargo. Dante's Atlantic Ulysses is no longer able to feel the size of the Mediterranean that continually restrains the sea with the earth. He is a man who has lost all sense of the dwelling. Wandering without *horizons* has become his way of life. He is even devoid of any memory of a home to which he might return to enjoy a break. The brother of Captain Ahab, Dante's Ulysses, who is the precursor of pirates, of whalers, and of the great ocean navigator Columbus, is a tragic figure of the will to power of a form of knowledge without limits or restraint.

Nietzsche: The New Columbus

Nietzsche dedicated a poem to Columbus in the summer of 1882, after spending the winter in Genoa. It was not by chance that the work was titled *Columbus Novus*:

> That's the way I want to go, and I trust
> Myself from now on and my grip!
> Open is the sea: into the blue
> Sails my Genoese ship.
> Everything becomes new and newer to me
> Behind me lies Genoa.
> Courage! You yourself stand at the helm,
> Dearest Victoria![17]

Even though, like many Germans, he felt the charm of the South, the sun, and the Mediterranean Sea, on whose shores he loved to winter, there is no doubt that Nietzsche was the philosopher who best understood the challenge of the open sea and heard the call of the ocean. For him, philosophers become "aeronauts of the spirit,"[18] or "brave birds which fly out into the distance, into the farthest distance," pushing further and further into the sea of knowledge, in that direction "where everything is sea, sea, sea!"[19] As they "*cross* the sea," they are animated by a mighty longing, which "is worth more to us than any pleasure"[20]—the inexhaustible thirst for knowledge that is finally free and no longer under any constraint. The same passion drives Dante's Ulysses and these aeronauts, who trust only in themselves and in their own rudders. It is the same desire to attain knowledge that establishes their route, and it is the same courage that they all have in common. In a similar vein to Ulysses and Columbus, they, too, orientate themselves "thither where all the suns of humanity have hitherto *gone down* [. . .] *steering westward.*"[21] They, too, chase the setting sun; they are ready for sunset, as long as the dawn of a new morning rises. They are aware of running the risk of being "wrecked against infinity."[22] And never did it seem so "sweet" to be shipwrecked in this sea!

But who are these reckless adventurers of thought, for whom the call of the ocean is irresistible? They are the new philosophers, those who have freed themselves from God, accepting his death without regret but rather with the boldness of one who foresees a new dawn. Nietzsche's aphorism 343, which opens the fifth book of *The Gay Science*, is revealingly titled "We Fearless Ones": "Finally the horizon seems clear again, even if not bright; finally our ships may set out again, set out to face any danger; every daring of the lover of knowledge is allowed again; the sea, our sea, lies open again; maybe there has never been such an 'open' sea."[23]

It is not an inland sea, a *mesógeos*. Rather, this *mare nostrum* is now a boundless, free, *open* sea; it is no longer contained by any shore; there is no land that delineates its edges. The wide marine expanse that opens up before these intrepid sailors does not unfold its space between any known lands. Nor does it touch any coast, nor can any port offer rest and shelter. The ship that plows through this smooth surface resolutely leaves behind every mooring, as well as every pier; no anchor can now hold it back or even reach the bottom: "Never before has a deeper world of insight opened up to bold travellers and adventurers."[24] We must therefore always go *forward* and always go *further*; we must "hold on tight to the

8 GEOPHILOSOPHY OF THE MEDITERRANEAN

helm,"[25] since there are no longer fixed stars to orient us along our path. There is only the obsessive fixation of a gaze that knows one direction—that of continuous *overcoming*. As Ulysses's progeny, the new philosophers—that is, the philosophers of the future—share with the Greek hero a certain capacity for dissimulation, although it is now completely put to the service of that passionate desire for knowledge, that *curiositas* that characterizes Dante's Ulysses: "Our adventurer's courage, our sly and pampered curiosity, our finest, stealthiest, most spiritual will to power and world-overcoming that greedily roams and revels throughout all the realms of the future."[26] The *innatus cognitionis amor*, the inborn love of knowledge that makes him *sapientiae cupidus*, a lover of wisdom, brings Nietzsche's new philosopher close to the Ulysses of Cicero, who was probably one of Dante's sources. But this yearning for knowledge has now become the *will* to know, *Wille zur Macht* as knowledge,[27] which can be stopped by no obstacle in its unrestrained course. No "mad flight" frightens it, as it has entirely forgotten any sense of limitation. The *Columbus Novus*—that is, the philosopher of the future—pays no more attention to the End point that is imposed on his journey. The columns of Hercules, faithful guardians of an obsolete measurement of the Mediterranean, are now completely emptied of any symbolic value. "On to the ships, you philosophers!"[28]—this is the mandatory invitation to get out to sea that Nietzsche launches to the thinkers of the future. He incites them to discover more than a new world in the "ocean of becoming."[29] He urges them to transform themselves into "adventurers and birds of passage," to look alert and be attentive and ready to steal everything that falls under their gaze "as sharply and as inquisitively as possible."[30] He longs to venture alongside them "out over the ocean, no less proud than the ocean itself."[31] These oceanic, Atlantic men, these daredevil heroes of knowledge are those "aeronauts of the spirit" who swarm from Old Europe, like migratory birds taking off for new and more hospitable shores, knowing that no land can be a safe home from now on but only a small foothold from which to fly even farther. Perhaps no Nietzschean passage is able to grasp the meaning of this dangerous crossing more effectively than the famous aphorism 124 of *The Gay Science*, titled "In the Horizon of the Infinite":

> We have forsaken the land and gone to sea! We have destroyed the bridge behind us—more so, we have demolished the land behind us! Now, little ship, look out! Beside you is the ocean; it is true, it does not always roar, and at times it lies there like silk and gold and dreams of goodness. But there will be hours when you realize that it is infinite and that there is nothing more awesome than infinity. Oh, the poor bird that has felt free and now strikes against the walls of this cage! Woe, when homesickness for the land overcomes you, as if there had been more freedom there—and there is no more "land"![32]

Far from being a *nóstos*, a homecoming, the journey Nietzsche conceives is genuinely an *éxodos*, a sailing with no return. No longer a *póntos*, this sea forces us to cut all bridges, to erase even the land that we leave behind forever. Now the ship becomes the one and only precarious abode for those who feel they have embarked, leaving behind only a trail drawn on the water, which quickly disappears. Everywhere there is the ocean, an immense expanse of water with no more land on the horizon. The gaze is always trained forward, persistently following the bow that makes its way along unknown routes. The ocean is *infinite, unlimited,* and without recognizable boundaries, an immense space devoid of measure, but, precisely for this reason, precisely because it is homogeneous and empty, it is extraordinarily willing to accept the measures that humans seek to impose on it. A horror vacui, a fear of emptiness and dismay in front of the Nothing, might then surprise these daring sailors, as there is nothing more frightening than feeling oneself slipping into this smooth expanse devoid of any nomos, of any law. Here, in the open, wide space of the sea, the pain of returning might assail sailors. They may well yearn for the land from which they turned away after finally making a decision to leave. But it would

10 GEOPHILOSOPHY OF THE MEDITERRANEAN

be futile to give in to this extreme, regressive temptation, as if the earth with its nomoi could still guarantee more freedom than the infinitely free space that the sea can now offer. It is impossible to go back to that land, which has been submerged by an ocean wave that now permeates everything. Like the ocean, it is now subject to a nihilistic *Ent-ortung*—a delocalization and a deterritorialization that no longer permits us to make roots or dwellings. How might one return to that land, how to return to that Mediterranean Sea that washed over it, if everything now appears as a tabula rasa of infinite oceanic expanse?

Remembering the Mediterranean

Nietzsche, who defined himself as a posthumous and untimely thinker, knew that his writings were not for his contemporaries but for posterity, for those who would live at least two centuries after him. He was writing for us, who have just entered the twenty-first century. No one has been able to describe our present circumstances with greater clarity or to foresee the inescapable decision that awaits us. Are we still, can we still call ourselves Mediterranean, or has this sea on which stormy winds blow definitively lost its historical centrality? Are we perhaps about to become, if we are not already, Atlantics—that is, fearless ocean navigators? Ever since the "discovery" of America and the first circumnavigations of the globe, have we entered the age that Schmitt called the "globale Zeit," the global epoch? In fact, where does the process of globalization come from, if not from that powerful yet provoking call caused by the first opening of the ocean in the era of great geographical discoveries? It was the era of Columbus and of pirates and whalers. Like great cetaceans, they were all free to undertake routes that had never before been attempted in an open sea without borders, resistant to any nomos. It is this same appeal that caused England, an island of rustic sheep farmers, to go to the sea: "Then the island turned its gaze away from the continent and raised it to the great seas of the world. It undocked and became the vehicle of an oceanic world empire."[33] Like a ship setting sail, this unanchoring (*Entankerung*) led the island to journey along the ocean routes until it founded, on this unsteady expanse, its mobile empire. But only America, the New World, was able to truly embody that oceanic spirit that England had inaugurated. The great continent did on a grand scale what the small island had only just begun. Ever since its inception, it became an extraordinary experiment in the practice of the Limitless. From the very beginning, it was unable to draw boundaries, to mark borders, other than as an ever-moving line of progress that is always on the point of being moved farther. The pioneer, this new pirate figure, was the undisputed hero of the conquest, not so much, and not only, of the immense prairies that opened like the ocean as far as the eye could see but rather of the West—that is, of a direction, a *route* westward, the same as for Dante's Ulysses. The pioneer succeeded, however, in accomplishing and carrying out that "mad" task that had ended in the shipwreck for Ulysses.

Now this ocean has become a *universe*, it has become a world under the sign of a flat and uniform universalism that is like the smooth expanse of a sea that knows no land, which has erased borders and, thereby, all possibilities of confrontation and dialogue that are respectful of differences. This world, now unified and rendered uniform by the global era, this oceanic world empire, far from guaranteeing perpetual peace, is like a shock wave that produces increasingly ungovernable wars and conflicts. Equally shapeless and immeasurable are the attempts at reterritorialization, including the all-out defense of identity and belonging. The world, therefore, ends up becoming ever more regressive and archaic.

The Mediterranean, however, is a *memory* of another story. It is an experience that is unique in the world, of the encounter between sea and land; it is a space for sharing that both separates and divides but also connects and unites. It favors exchanges between identities that, in their incessant confrontation, desire to remain different. In its plurality of borders and frontiers, it has been a space of clashes but also of extraordinary encounter, of inexhaustible confrontation with the other, preventing or moderating any drastic *reductio ad unum*, reduction to one. From this sea of differences, Europe was born. It is an irreducible *pluri*verse of peoples and languages that are forced to dialogue with one another, forced into an eternal translation and distancing. Will this ancient sea surrounded by lands know how to be a model now for a world not *uni*versal but *pluri*versal? Will we all—and not just we Europeans—be able to become Mediterranean once again and finally find a new nomos, a new measure, between heaven, earth, and sea?

Two

Europe to Come

> Will this Evening-Land, rising above Occident and Orient and transcending the European, become the place of the coming, more primordially destined, history?
>
> —Martin Heidegger, *Anaximander's Saying*

> World history travels from east to west; for Europe is the absolute end of history, just as Asia is the beginning.
>
> —Georg Wilhelm Friedrich Hegel, *Lectures on the Philosophy of World History*

Europe in Crisis

In ancient Greece, in that narrow strip of land that juts out into the Mediterranean, some men in the seventh and sixth century BC began to question the world around them with a new attitude. They called this new theoretical outlook "philosophy," as they preferred a disinterested type of universal knowledge.[1] From that decisive moment in the course of human history began a bimillenary adventure of rationality: after many unexpected twists and turns, its final result emerged as that "calculative thinking" that first asserted itself in Europe at the beginning of the modern age. This way of thinking now constitutes the unique and all-pervading thought that dominates the entire terrestrial globe unchallenged. The process of westernization of the world[2] is nothing but a rampant affirmation of the imperatives of a technical-scientific-economic rationality, born on European soil, which everywhere imposes its own model of rationalization, homologation, and drastic reduction of any qualitative differences to mere quantitative differences that are easily measured and calculated. Faced with the devastating results of this violent reduction of thought to domination and calculation of the real, the need for a de-cision and a reversal has arisen. The major philosophers of the twentieth century—from Heidegger to Jünger, from Levinas to Derrida—did not shirk from the task. We must be able to oppose this expanding desert of technical-economic nihilism by sharing new perspectives and taking different approaches in order to "think otherwise." How, then, would a geophilosophical reconsideration of Europe look—namely, a reconsideration of its controversial identity and destiny in light of the new global challenges to which it is called to respond?

After all the events that have upset the structure and the previous equilibrium of our continent, it is difficult to say whether to categorize the disturbances that have appeared across Europe as a type of birth or just an agony. On the other hand, it is "proper" to Europe (and its inhabitants) to be perpetually in crisis, to be able to criticize and radically contradict itself, to be reborn each time from its own ashes as the same and yet somehow different. That is a "property" that exposes Europe to an eternal self-expropriation.

There is no need to rehearse familiar discourses about the difficulties Europe has faced in its various attempts to define itself. Nor do we need to be reminded of the precious and indispensable experience on its soil of the cohabitation of a plurality of peoples and different traditions who have been able to find various forms and methods of dialogue, all while safeguarding their own inherent individuality. Although the plurality of Europe means that it lacks any *one* particular identity, as many of its roots are incompatible with one another (Greek, Latin, Germanic, Jewish, Christian, Islamic, and so on), it nevertheless should have resulted in an idyllic harmonious coexistence among peoples who respect each other's

EUROPE TO COME

identities in the name of a model of civilization and humanity whose claim to universality Europe has imposed on the rest of the world either by force or persuasion. In fact, this "spiritual" Europe, which aims to embody universal values of humanism as well as economic and social well-being, has an attraction that is difficult to escape. This idea of Europe as the "cradle of civilization," and of a Western tradition that conquered the world by presenting itself as a "universal value" in the name of the universal human rights, is, nevertheless, replete with glaring contradictions.

Any comforting image of Europe has been spoiled by anomalies like Nazism, which is a stain on our memory and still awaits fuller consideration. Nazism was certainly not extraneous to European culture and its "values." More recently, this image of Europe has been spoiled by the difficult task of defending its integrity and identity against new migratory flows that threaten to break through its borders on a daily basis, provoking xenophobic reactions, local outcry, and racial hatred. Europe appears to be almost surprised or dismayed by these disturbing and recurring problems within its "civil" confines—problems that Europe believed had become a thing of the past. It seems incapable of recognizing the return of its own repressed past. In the wake of an unprecedented financial crisis, it is equally unable to react effectively in any resolute way. Its response requires real political unification, which has until now always been postponed for some later date. Europe today is a proper name[3] that lacks any concrete geopolitical space that would enable it to become a credible interlocutor either internally, between the various federal states that constitute it, or externally, on the global scene. It will never really see the light unless it questions the foundation of its own existence once again, asking itself how its manifold features can find a form.

An increasing centripetal movement conveys knowledge and decisions to a few key places (Brussels, Strasbourg, Berlin, Paris), forcing the peripheries to "suffer" them. Predictably, a forceful, antagonistic countermovement has been developing. It emerges in the individual territories whose residents claim decision-making power and the right to be heard, all while demanding to "participate" in the choices. The Europe of banks, financial powers, bureaucracies, and glass buildings seems increasingly removed from its local territories and communities, which demand to be included in the decisions that directly affect them and shape their existence. This Europe is characterized by capital and by the neoliberal ideology, which is a new belief system and one way of thinking from right to left. Its opposite would be a socially supportive type of Europe that places the logic of the common good before the logic of profit and the interest of all before the interest of the individual.

Europe is unable to decide where it should turn its gaze: toward the Baltic or toward the Mediterranean? toward the East, that is, toward what was once the Soviet empire? or toward the West, beyond the Atlantic? Should it cling even closer to its "historical" ally, the mighty American empire? or turn instead toward the far south, toward the North African coasts of the Mediterranean, where ferments and hopes of a new democratic awakening are emerging?

The questions are endless, as is the list of countless indecisions that paralyze Europe. It is for this reason that the time has come to make choices that can no longer be postponed if we are to prevent the excessive power of forces and determined interests from gaining the upper hand. They are sometimes hidden under the guise of demands made by technocrats and often sound like genuine ultimatums that only *seem* indisputable.

But to find answers to these questions and choose an appropriate pathway among all those available, it is first necessary to reflect on Europe itself—not only on its history but on its very beginning, exploring the complex melting pot of ideas from which it arose and on which its survival and future depend.

Finis Europae

Europe is at the beginning. Europe is at the beginning because with Europe *begins* the history of globalization, which started as the Europeanization of the world in the colonial age and then took the form of a westernization of the world when the United States of America assumed the role of undisputed power worldwide (this is why westernization is, above all, an Americanization of the world). But Europe is also always at the beginning of itself, in a perennial gestation; it is always on the verge of being born or reborn from its own rubble. A powerful geophilosophical image has imposed itself across the world: that of a small cape of the Asian continent that has reached out to show itself as *caput mundi*, head of the world. From Nietzsche to Valéry, and from Heidegger to Schmitt and Derrida,[4] the beginning and the end of Europe and its ultimate fulfilment cannot detach themselves from the shape of this small strip of land that advances into the sea, leaving the vast continent behind. Europe, as "cape" and head of the whole world, has radiated its spiritual strength everywhere, expanding its borders to excess. It first became America, the New World, in contrast to the old continent from which the first enterprising pioneers departed. Then it became the West, whose meaning now has a global and planetary significance that stretches far beyond the Western Hemisphere. Whether we like it or not, in the time that Europe has existed, Time has become our time—the time of the West. That is to say, the very History of the world. At least, this is what we have had the presumption to think, and we have firmly believed it to be the case. We have so forcefully and incessantly proclaimed this as a truth that the whole world has become the westernization of the world.

But this same process has also brought about its end.

Europe is at the end. There are many clues that suggest the end of Europe. Its inevitable decline has, for a long time now, been announced by many. Today, it has become more evident than ever that the profound economic crisis that shakes Europe to its very core is perhaps the fatal blow to the long, exhausting agony of a sick body whose disease is slowly destroying it. In fact, Europe, which was once the driving force of the world, now occupies a peripheral place next to the American colossus and new emerging powers.

Europe, which is always in crisis and in search of itself, must continually question itself through a self-reflection of which even our discussion is a part.

Which Europe must then thrive, and which is destined to fade away?

In the last century, Europe has felt finished and aspired to a rebirth several times. The first was in the immediate aftermath of World War I, when national monarchies and the last empire (the Hapsburgs) collapsed. This structure had maintained the unity of Europe within the order of *jus publicum europaeum* throughout the modern age. But it was not a final collapse: an interregnum opened up, replete with uncertainty and catastrophic forebodings, as is apparent from Oswald Spengler's *Decline of the West*.[5] Although they took different approaches, many thinkers, such as Husserl, Jaspers, Heidegger, Jünger, and Schmitt, among others, uttered their diagnosis and prescribed possible remedies at the bedside of the great patient. Their response to the disease and its source was quite unanimous. As Nietzsche had already prophesied at the end of the previous century, "nihilism stands at the door: whence comes this uncanniest of all guests?"[6] It is a particularly insidious disease since, far from presenting itself as such, it instead manifests itself through an excessive vigor and health. It takes on the appearance of a technical-economic domain whose effects are so miraculous as to assume the idolatrous features of a new faith and a new religion. But a more careful diagnosis sees behind this disruptive vitality and notices a symptom of a weakening of the spirit that attacks Europe not from the outside but from its own inside, itself the most mature fruit of European civilization. Like two buboes, two world wars exploded in rapid succession to tear the body apart.

The search for a nomos, for a law, became an unavoidable task, which is yet to be completed, to impose a new order on European soil, which had been deeply disrupted by the two conflicts, along with the rest of the world, which was bereft of its center. According to the sharp and foreseeing diagnosis of Carl Schmitt,[7] the Eurocentric nomos of the earth, which had emerged after the discovery of the New World, had now been definitively destroyed. For almost four hundred years, this order—based on a balance between the land and sea—had arranged the entire planet, starting from the formation of the nation-States on European soil and including the dominance of the English empire along oceanic routes.

The two world wars were an unprecedented form of combat that will transform every clash after them into a "world civil war." Afterward, not only were the monarchies defeated but so also was the State-form itself, which was condemned to an irreversible sunset. The world was divided into two large hemispheres dominated by the two great empires that had been victorious over the German Reich: the United States of America and the Soviet Union. But it was an unstable equilibrium, founded on terror, which soon gave way, with the fall of the Berlin Wall and the collapse of the Soviet empire, to that unity of the world we call globalization.

The imperial dream of Hitler's National Socialism was the ultimate attempt to give Europe a new order, albeit in a completely delusional form. Even before the Allies' bombing raids, Europe was shipwrecked in the extermination camps, where an entire people were suppressed because they were deemed unworthy of being part of the human race. At the top of that race were the Aryans, who reared their terrifying heads in the horror of the crematoria, where millions of victims, guilty only of being *others*, were sacrificed. It is in this apocalyptic scenario, during the "last days of mankind," that the project of a Nazi and racist Europe collapses into the darkness from which it arose. Auschwitz[8] is the name of this precipice, of this abyss that, like a caesura, tears apart European history, breaking and abruptly busting its continuum. For this reason, Auschwitz is still the last but also the first word in this indelible memory of a wound that, for Europe, is always open.

Evening-Land and Morning-Land

Faced with the apocalyptic landscape that opened up at the end of World War II, it was not difficult to acknowledge that we had arrived at the end of an era. In Geneva, in 1946, some leading intellectuals of the various European countries met to discuss the "European spirit."[9] They sought to investigate the causes that led

20   GEOPHILOSOPHY OF THE MEDITERRANEAN

to the catastrophe and to try to plan for the future. The German philosopher Karl Jaspers was called upon. He renewed hopes for a "spiritual Europe" and its humanistic values that would be open to other cultures, including those of the East. In the same year, Heidegger wrote "Anaximander's Saying" and gave the lecture "Why Poets?,"[10] which he dedicated to Rilke on the twentieth anniversary of the poet's death. Heidegger raised far more radical questions about the fate of the West. Rather than turning our attention to the "beautiful souls" of old Europe, it is by questioning thinkers who are in many ways considered to be "awkward" that we will be able to learn more about the abyss into which Europe had fallen at the end of World War II and to understand whether it is destined to fade away. Thinkers like Heidegger, Jünger, and Schmitt did not sidestep the most controversial issues of their time, and it was inevitable that their work would be set aside in the immediate postwar period.

As early as the summer semester of 1935, Heidegger announced in one of his university courses[11] that there was a "darkening of the world" that now encompasses the whole earth. It manifests itself in what Hölderlin had called "the flight of the gods" or in Nietzsche's image of the expanding desert, in the devastation of the earth, and in the standardization of humanity. It is the triumph of that "reign of quantity" that René Guénon discussed in an important 1945 publication.[12] The darkening of the world contains within itself "a *disempowering of the spirit* [*Entmachtung des Geistes*], its dissolution, diminution, suppression, and misinterpretation."[13] It shows itself as a blindness that primarily concerns Europe, which is "always on the point of cutting its own throat."[14] It is caught in the grip between Russia and America, which, despite their apparent antagonism, "seen metaphysically, are both the same: the same hopeless frenzy of unchained technology and of the rootless organization of the average man."[15] But the most insidious trait of this crisis is, in Heidegger's eyes, the fact that "the spiritual decline of the earth has progressed so far that people are in danger of losing their last spiritual strength, the strength that makes it possible even to see

EUROPE TO COME

the decline [. . .] and to appraise it as such."[16] Therefore, to understand this *such* decline, as Heidegger adds in parentheses, means to relate it to the destiny of Being. For this reason, all speeches on the "decline of the West," as well as the hopes of a spiritual rebirth, do not grasp the essence of the European crisis, because they are unable to see beyond a purely historiographical approach instead of reconnecting it to that history of Being (*Seins-Geschichte*) that Heidegger, following Nietzsche, was able to recognize as *nihilism*. It is only by beginning from this *ontological* perspective that Heidegger can state: "Our own hour is the era of downgoing [*Untergang*]. The down-going [*Unter-gang*], in the essential sense, is the path [*Gang*] to the reticent preparation for what is to come. [. . .] This downgoing is the utterly first beginning. [. . .] Only those who belong can know the era of down-going. All others must fear the down-going and thus deny and renounce it, for to them it is sheer weakness and mere ending."[17] It is in this gap between a historiographical analysis (political, sociological, anthropological, economic, etc.) and a philosophical-ontological approach that we can fully appreciate the distance that separates Heidegger's diagnosis from conventional discourses on the "European spirit", which are still redundant today. Moreover, the blindness of Europe and its misunderstanding comes from itself. It is a self-cutting, or self-annihilation: "The situation of Europe is all the more dire because the disempowering of the spirit comes from Europe itself."[18] Ernst Jünger, in his celebrated 1932 monograph *Der Arbeiter*,[19] had, for his part, shown how European soil had become the scene of a now-decisive clash between the Bourgeois and his worn-out values, among which economic interest reigned supreme, and that new human Figure—the Jüngerian variation of the Nietzschean overman—who was forged on the battlefields of World War I. This new individual is the Worker, who is the only one truly capable of tapping into and dominating the elemental force. For this very reason, the Worker is endowed with an extraordinary shaping power. Heidegger does not share Jünger's initial enthusiasm for this Figure but nevertheless agrees with his rejection of the rhetoric and nostalgia for a European "humanism,"

22 GEOPHILOSOPHY OF THE MEDITERRANEAN

which both view as having irrevocably waned.[20] Instead, he intends to patiently interrogate the internal process that has led to this end, and, with a resolute determination, he seeks to fully explore the meaning of this twilight, beyond any optimistic or pessimistic forecasts. As Nietzsche had already suggested, Heidegger believes that it is necessary to welcome the decline, to go through it completely and touch its depths, in order to get to the other side and prepare for another new beginning.[21] But what are the traits that characterize the declining European spirit? In them is reflected that nihilism that runs through all Western thought ever since its first Platonic beginning as "metaphysics"—namely, the oblivion of Being and its truth, which ultimately reveals itself in that "mobilization" of all beings that everywhere opens the way to the desert: "The decline of the truth of beings occurs necessarily, and indeed as the completion of metaphysics. The decline occurs through the collapse of the world characterized by metaphysics, and at the same time through the desolation of the earth stemming from metaphysics."[22] These words are taken from "Overcoming Metaphysics," a series of reflections noted between 1936 and 1946, crucial years for the destiny of Europe. These words are echoed by those of "Anaximander's Saying," a text that dates to 1946:

> Are we the latecomers of a history that now speeds toward its end, an end in which everything terminates in an ever more desolate ordering of uniformity? [. . .] Do we stand in the very twilight of the most monstrous transformation of the whole earth and of the time of the historical space in which it is suspended? Do we stand before the evening of the night of another dawn? Are we setting forth on a journey into the historical land of the earth's evening? Is the Land of the Evening [*Land des Abends*] only now emerging? Will this Evening-Land [*Abend-Land*], rising above Occident and Orient and transcending the European, become the place of the coming, more primordially destined, history? Are we men of today already "Western" in a sense that first arises out of our passage into the world's night?[23]

It is only by fully fulfilling that "destiny" which is the West (*Abendland*), when Europe will be able to recognize itself as that Evening-Land (*Abend-Land*) that it was destined to become, that it will be possible "to go forth to meet the coming decisions to become, perhaps and in a wholly other mode, a land of dawn, an Orient."[24] In the general disorientation that characterizes the Western European human being as nomadic and uprooted, Heidegger does not think of new roots in *Blut und Boden*, in blood and soil. Rather, he thinks, *beyond* the decline, of the event of a land of dawn, of a *new land*.[25] It is a land that is fully Western precisely for being able to look at its own "Orient" as it turns toward the enigma of its first great beginning. Heidegger only offers us uncertain traces and, possibly, paths of thinking our way into this Land, or this other Europe. In the face of Europe's globalization, when Europe paradoxically gets lost at the precise moment of its extension across the planet, Heidegger does not provide easy predictions or answers. Rather, he constantly poses new questions:

> The humble is the occidental. Greece, however, the oriental, is the great beginning that may possibly come. The humble *is*, however, only insofar as it *becomes* that to which the great beginning can come. Can it still come? Does the occidental still exist? It has become Europe. Europe's technological-industrial domination has already covered the entire earth. On the other hand, the earth, as a planet, has already been included in the interstellar-cosmic space which is placed at man's disposal by the planned projects of man.[26]

Will we be able to live up to these questions?

The Event of Europe

In the first half of the twentieth century, all thinking had focused on the issue of the fate of Europe, on which the very fate of the West depended. It was for this reason that intellectuals, philosophers, and writers entered into the discussion,[27] long before professional politicians or financial and economic experts. The postwar partition of the world into two opposing blocs not only introduced unprecedented forms of conflict such as the Cold War but also exacerbated and reduced the complexity of those reflections into a schematic ideological contrast. Like a Siberia of thought, a glaciation of the spirit, this partition has frozen the world order in its icy grip for over forty years, paralyzing history and stopping the course of its seasons in a single long winter. On the one hand, it has erased memories, identities, and traditions. On the other, it has prevented Europe from independent growth. The thaw, which began with perestroika, finally overwhelmed the banks in 1989 with the fall of the Berlin Wall. After this hibernation, much of the world experienced a great upheaval that accelerated the course of history, which had seemed blocked. Again, there was a feeling that we had reached the end of an era, but also that there was finally another Europe beginning. The collapse of communism, especially in the eastern countries, imposed a new geography and new borders as well as new definitions. Once again, Germany felt called upon to play a decisive role. There were, however, unexpected problems. These included the revitalization of ethnic groups and new nationalisms, Islamic fundamentalism and its threatening expansionism, international terrorism, and renewed American imperialism, accompanied by new "humanitarian" wars to export democracy. There were also uncontrollable waves of migration from neighboring countries and from non-EU countries. Then there was an alarming ecological crisis. All these problems dampened easy enthusiasm since Europe was completely unprepared to face them.

The answers that have been given up to now cannot fail to appear disappointing, if not laughable, when seen in light of the challenge we face in our own time. Currently, it is mainly politicians and "experts," bureaucrats and bankers who discuss Europe. There is now a need to deal with a world market that has become uncontrollable, whose cyclical crises require corrective measures that do not have the courage to cure the disease at its root; rather, they aggravate it. Europe, this new Europe that has yet to come, if it ever

EUROPE TO COME

comes, will not come from the unbridled freedom of the market. Rather, it will only emerge from an unforeseen, unpredictable *event*. Nevertheless, it is up to us, as a task, to prepare for this event. If there ever is a future for Europe, it cannot fail to happen as the *event of the other*, as the promise of a decisive turning point for history. Europe must not simply be revived or, worse, resurrected. Between preservation of memory and preparation for the future, it must first of all become a space of openness and welcome *its* other, "which is not, never was, and never will be Europe."[28] It must be an openness that does not simply assimilate the other to itself, along the lines of any harmful notion of "integration." Moreover, being open prevents Europe from any focus on itself, any reappropriation of itself and its own identity.

As Derrida remarked, "*what is proper to a culture is to not be identical to itself.*"[29] It is only by starting from this assumption that we can truly prepare for the event of another Europe, of a Europe to-come. This event, however, at its bottom, is incalculable and unforeseeable. There can therefore be no feasible planning since it will concern a decision and a responsibility that exceeds every possible forecast and calculation. What engages us in this task is the paradox that calls us to enter into a double bind: on the one hand, we must be guardians of a tradition that has made Europe *unique* in comparison to all other countries, without considering it as a legacy to be archived and capitalized. On the other hand, we must open Europe's past to what it has never been but could become, while not emphasizing the new, or the absolutely different, at the risk of fatally succumbing to total amnesia. Preparing a future for Europe primarily means recognizing ourselves as its heirs but not in the obvious sense of this word. It is not simply that we will receive an inheritance; rather, we must freely and responsibly receive that which was destined for us. It is for us to testify and answer for it for the future. Being heirs then involves a paradoxical task, but it is our only one: we must safeguard, defend, and protect the gifts of our memory, and, at the same time, we must open ourselves to the gift of the other, to the stranger, to the unfamiliar, to the foreigner, who should be fully recognized for his, her, its, or their radical heterogeneity and irreducible otherness.[30] Thus, we must reject both the conciliatory and engulfing logic of integration and that of tolerance, which negates the other as other: neither one nor the other opens that space, that necessary distance, that *difference* that is indispensable so that, in the encounter and in the welcome, the unique individuality of every person can be safeguarded and preserved.

Perhaps it is even *impossible* to fully obey these two laws. Perhaps we cannot be faithful to our memory and welcome the other. Perhaps no "law" on hospitality will ever be able to satisfy the demands of this welcome. Yet it is only from this "impossible" premise that the promise of a future for Europe can reach us. Indeed, it is only on this horizon that real responsibility is given, when one exposes oneself to the possibility of the impossible, where the simple execution of a plan or project, however scrupulously conceived, can transform morality and politics into pure technology, which is *always* irresponsible, or, worse, into a mask. There is no calculation or rule to prepare for Europe to-come, and for this reason the "technocrats" alone will never be able to "invent" it; rather, it is a question of *responsibility*, in the sense of having to answer for Europe, for an idea of Europe, which, coming from the other, is always indebted to the other.

Starting from this responsibility, it is a question of thinking differently the Stranger and the Foreigner, as well as the Familiar. We must also think differently about limits, borders, and frontiers, not only in geographical and political terms but also in their cultural meanings.[31] If up to now they have been determined by the Same, how would we define them now, starting from the Other? How should we safeguard a tradition (land, language, religion, ethnic group, etc.) without it degenerating into particularism, racism, fundamentalism, fanaticism? How might we open up this tradition to the Stranger without distorting it or making it lose its specific character? without effacing that which makes it unique in the name of a misunderstood principle of translatability and homologating universality? Which idea of translation, of transit, of passage—not only of one language into another—must be accepted so that the

Another Europe

singularity and uniqueness of each idiom is preserved in its own untranslatability while nevertheless facilitating a certain degree of translation?

Another Europe

Nothing is more elusive and, at the same time, more compelling than the idea of Europe. As has often been noted, Europe has never had clearly delineated geographical borders, nor a single language or culture. The various political forms that have occurred on its territory created unifications around different centers. They have continually shifted Europe's focus, and they have also caused significant tensions between the West and East, as in, for example, the antagonism between Rome and Byzantium, or between North and South, under the sign of a Germanic or Latin empire. There have also been tensions between adherents to different religious beliefs: Catholics, Protestants, Orthodox Christians, Jews, and Muslims. Europe has therefore always been one and many, never identical to itself, if not starting from the innumerable differences that give shape to it. Its long and troubled journey in search of itself—that movement that we have described as incessant un-definition—therefore starts from a plural identity, which is *different in itself* from the very beginning. Since its inception, there has been a Europe that identifies itself with the West *against* the East, with the North *against* the South, and with *ratio* (reason or rationality) *against* any other form of thought. But the fact of the matter is that these contradictions do not threaten Europe from the outside; they have always tormented Europe internally. Europe has been infinitely torn and divided from within, and this has prevented it from suturing these wounds once and for all into a reconciled identity. Its darkest moments were perhaps when this identity managed to show itself *as a whole*. Being unable to access any fixed identity, however, does not entail an absence of a clearly defined singularity. Europe challenges us to grasp it precisely in its divisions and conflicts, as well as in the differences that have always characterized it. It demonstrates in the best way that every identity constitutes itself as an irreconcilable difference. It is not that this otherness belongs to a reassuring outside against which we might want to measure ourselves: every dialectical identity either expels and rejects the other from itself or "works" it by assimilating it to itself, to the point of eliminating its irreducible difference, showing it finally reconciled and "sedated" in a superior unity. Rather, identity always starts from the other without ever being able to resolve the other and dissolve the other in itself, unless through unprecedented violence. Europe has been the testing ground, and yet it still seems not to have understood this. A serious de-cision awaits Europe, a choice between alternatives that seem irreconcilable; the fate of the West, on which the fate of the whole world now depends, may also depend on its answer. This de-cision, which therefore involves the fate of the whole planet, requires the *responsibility* of knowing how to *respond* to the provocations and demands of the present. The latter everywhere challenges us through the unsettling imposition of a technical-economic-financial apparatus, which is expressed in the imperatives of techno-science and a market that is now completely out of control since it only values profit and money. This plan, which first occurred in Europe, then in America, and finally in the world, has become our *destiny*. The westernization of the world, which started from Europe, is almost complete. It has created a "new world order" that is no longer Eurocentric but revolves, increasingly in the West, around a new *Axis Mundi*, a new world axis that is North America. In the future, it will probably move farther West, toward China and India, in unprecedented but still "Western" forms. Perhaps by turning to the old continent another Europe could arise, beyond East and West and their historical features?

Technical-scientific-economic rationality is an extreme form of domination over the world that pursues its conquest on a planetary scale in a way that is less conspicuous and yet far more pervasive and violent than its colonial predecessor, since its promise of well-being and happiness takes on an unparalleled power of seduction. Faced with the unification of the world as a fait accompli,[32] the ancient

EUROPE TO COME

political alternatives of the Right and the Left seem to collapse; they no longer hold up, like the wall between Russia and the United States, an iron curtain that took just one breath to demolish.

But then, in the ever-increasing uniformization of the globe, is there still space, is there still time for that event we call "Europe"? Can something like Europe still take place in the tabula rasa of the planetary desert?

The hegemony of Euro-Western thought has imposed itself on the world under the guise of helping, forcing, obliging, and seducing others to become like us, who are the embodiment of humanity and the universal. In a terrifying heterogenesis of ends, the cradle of civilization, and tolerance of people, has caused the most frightening cultural genocides and the most desolate devastation of the planet. Its destructive power has impacted not only the colorful geography of its peoples but also nature in all its forms, living and nonliving. Animals, plants, millenary rocks, and entire landscapes have been annihilated, scarred, reduced to a bare desert by human beings—that is to say, a *certain* type of human being—and all in the name of their inalienable rights. Living species are silently consumed every day; they disappear, without us even noticing it, on earth, in the seas, and in the sky, like a gradual and invisible disease that slowly corrodes and dries up the world, while we grow and multiply at a dizzying pace, taking more and more space in the retreat of nature, becoming more and more equal and uniform, more and more similar to a mask that is deprived of the features of a face, in the progressive cancellation of every recognizable feature. This, however, does not happen without setbacks. Only within the nonpeaceful affirmation of this epochal loss of roots is it possible to understand the awakening of the need for identity and rootedness. It is at this level that a decisive battle will be fought for the fate of all humanity, because only by starting from our answers will we be able to overcome—or, perhaps, indefinitely prolong—the era of the "last man," as Nietzsche liked to call him. The rekindling of religious and ethnic wars to unthinkable levels of aggression disturbs the civilized world, and Europe in particular. It awakens the nightmares of times when, at the origins of modernity, Europe's soil was covered in blood by civil wars between Catholic and Protestant factions, and the ethnic cleansings evoke the horror of a past that cannot be archived, with their court of unprecedented violence and atrocities. A certain type of Islam has taken the place that real socialism has just left vacant. It is even more fundamentalist and totalitarian, and it has fueled international terrorism. Across the world, the poor begin to knock on our doors with increasingly thunderous blows. At any moment, they might break them down and tear down the barricades that we have used to lock them up. Europe feels threatened by the flood of this wave. It fears losing its integrity, which is already internally threatened by increasingly widespread autonomic and localistic pressures. It fears fragmentation, pulverization, perhaps even the cancellation and oblivion of its ancient traditions while nevertheless remaining mute and paralyzed in its impotence. On the one hand, "democratic" Europe preaches tolerance, integration, solidarity, and a harmoniously multiracial society that must be pacified in common adherence to democratic rules. On the other hand, even within its borders, there are racial hatreds, xenophobia, and demands for a strong identity that acts as a bulwark against any foreign invasion. An indigenous Europe is invoked that is identical to itself, closed in itself, without any subsidence toward the Foreigner. Often, contradictory answers are given to this complex scenario. On the one hand, there is the indefinite defense of the borders of each nation and of the State-form so that the identity of each country is preserved intact, as if these borders were not a mobile frontier fixed historically and geopolitically, as if the presumed identity of each European people were not the result of the continuous confrontation of each with the others and, internally, of the different populations that compose it. This defense is accompanied, paradoxically, with the idea of a European confederation that is capable of overcoming-preserving the borders of individual states but being unable to indicate a truly unitary *politics*. Rethinking all this does not mean finding retrospectives or future legitimations for Europe, which is still vague; it means, on the contrary, opening space for radical questions that can no longer wait about the need to change direction.

Europe to Come

The Europe of pluralism and tolerance, integration and dialogue, solidarity, human rights, and democracy against all forms of totalitarianism must take yet another stretch of road if it really wants to conceive of a coexistence capable of accounting for the singularity and irreducibility of everyone, for the radical determination of its here and now: space, time, sex, skin color, language, religious faith, and so on. How can we think of the singularity of these events without erasing it in wider identities and histories? Only by starting from the other do I find what I am and what I have to be. I must recognize my proximity to the Foreign, to the Stranger, and to the unfamiliar, not as something that threatens me but as that which constitutes me. So, it will be a question of recognizing in *oneself*—and not outside—that other to which we must respond and to which we are called to answer in the name of another Europe, of a Europe that is *unique* in the different faces that compose it without any of them defining it. From all these faces, from all these languages, a new image could take shape, as in a mosaic. It would be a Europe united in all its fragments, identical to itself only in that it is multiple and different in itself, held together by the inexhaustible desire of each to confront the other, in a dialogue fueled not by what is familiar and common but by what is and must remain absolutely foreign and singular.

Mediterranean Europe

Nevertheless, for Europe to rediscover that European "spirit" that has made it unique and unmistakable since its inception on Greek soil, it must first face a crucial dilemma. It must return, first of all, to rethink its origin, dissolving that ambiguous identification that allows it to assimilate itself to the West, that land of the waning sun in which the night's darkness makes everything indistinct and uniform.

Europe must again return to explore its history, which began on the shores of the Mediterranean, in Phoenicia, that extreme strip of land that delimits its border to the east. The story of

Zeus's kidnapping is in fact linked to the Mediterranean and its islands. The myth recalls that the god saw a beautiful girl with a "wide face," which is possibly an etymology for the word *Europe*. She was gathering flowers on the seashore near Tyre, and Zeus fell in love with her so deeply that he assumed the form of a docile white bull and decided to seduce her and drag her with him on a prodigious crossing of the sea to Crete, where, finally, transformed into an eagle, he joined her. It is therefore on the shores of the Mediterranean, among its jagged lands filled with ports and gulfs, promontories and islands, that the history of Europe speaks to us. It is here, in this sea that Europe crossed on that singular steed, that we can locate the ultimate meaning not only of the origin of Europe and the events of its history but also the events of its future. As the east coast and the crossing of the sea remind us of the youthful beauty of a Europe whose history is all included within the shores of the Mediterranean, so do the fatal attraction for the West and the call of the Ocean remind us of Europe's inexorable decline, in the mad crossing beyond Mediterranean borders in pursuit of the dying sun.

This is the dilemma that grips Europe, today more than ever: the decision that can no longer be postponed between those two souls that very soon began to tear it apart. There is that which binds Europe to its cradle and its origin—that is, the Mediterranean—and that which incessantly draws it beyond those confines perceived as too narrow and pushes it toward unknown, more open seas, toward the infinite free and empty space of the Ocean. The call of the Ocean, which is more irresistible than a siren song, attracts Europe and prompts it to embark on a journey that allows it to lose itself in the West, to set like the sun that goes down on the horizon. It prompts Europe to lose its focus, identifying itself only as the land of the waning sun, of the sunset, *Abend-Land*, or Evening-Land. Not from Tyre to Crete but from one side of the Atlantic to the other, this other prodigious crossing makes Europe forget the memory of its origin and hand it over to the destiny of the New World on which it lands. Hence the westernization of the world goes forward, forgetting the Mediterranean origin of Europe. Between these two different aquatic surfaces, between the flat ocean expanse of the Limitless and the intimate space of the Mediterranean, of a sea that is always held in check by land, there lies our decision about the destiny of Europe. Will we be able to go back to questioning the meaning of our history? Will we be able to remember what the Mediterranean means for us historically and geophilosophically?[33] The Mediterranean represents a unique experience of the encounter between sea and land, of a space of sharing that separates and divides but also connects and unites, favoring exchanges between identities that, in the incessant dialogue, prefer to remain different. In its plurality of borders and boundaries, it has been a place of conflict but also of extraordinary encounter and inexhaustible confrontation with the other, preventing and moderating any drastic *reductio ad unum*. From this sea of differences, Europe was born as an irreducible *pluri*verse of peoples and languages that are forced to dialogue with each other, forced into incessant translation. Will this ancient sea surrounded by land still be a model for a non-*universal* but *pluri*versal configuration of the world? Will we all—not just us Europeans—be able to become Mediterranean once again and finally find a new nomos, a new measure, between heaven, land, and sea?

Despite his attraction to the ocean, Nietzsche was also a Mediterranean thinker and certainly understood the Mediterranean vocation of Europe. He asserts in an 1885 fragment that was written in Sils-Maria, in the mountains of the much-loved Engadine:

> Rediscover the *south* in oneself and spread out above oneself a bright gleaming mysterious southern sky; reconquer one's southern health and the hidden might of the soul; step by step become more comprehensive, more supranational, more European, more supra-European, more eastern, finally *more Greek*—for the Greek was the first great bond and synthesis of everything eastern—and therewith the very *beginning* of the European soul, the

discovery *of our "new* world"—whoever lives under such imperatives, who knows what he can encounter some day? Perhaps even—*a new day!*[34]

Therefore, we, too, are waiting for this "new world" and the "new day" when Europe will finally be able to come.

Three

A Sea That Unites and Divides

A Sea Surrounded by Lands

It seems almost impossible to say anything more about the Mediterranean.[1] It is a topic that has been extensively studied in recent years and has a very rich bibliography. Despite ample research undertaken in various disciplines (including those outside the humanities), these studies are nevertheless, in many respects, a dead letter. The "Mediterranean question," which is extraordinarily rich in voices and approaches, seems to appeal more to intellectuals than to those who work in politics, who should nevertheless try to translate thought into action, especially where Europe is involved. Apart from a few broad policy outlines, the policies of the European community reflect a geopolitical outlook that is entirely focused on central Europe. Its outlook is toward the East on one side, where Europe encompasses the countries of the former Soviet Union. The other side is focused on the West, toward the ocean and the North American coast, which we now feel so close to that we might say that the Atlantic has become the new *mare nostrum*. Countries like Italy, who look out onto the southern shore toward the Mediterranean, seem to prefer to look away from the sea and turn their gaze upward, toward the North. The fact of the matter is that the Mediterranean has become a sea of problems for them more than for any other European country. Beyond the hopes of democracy (and of lucrative new business that consolidates old privileges) rekindled by the revolts in North Africa, the Mediterranean is, for the European continent, a pressing call to defend the security of its coastal borders, which are continually threatened and "transgressed" by new barbarian invasions,[2] by frequent arrivals of migrants who flee misery and violence and seek better living conditions.

The Mediterranean was first the sea of the Crusades and then a sea of cruises, first a sea of trade and commerce and then a sea of tourist and pleasure trips. Currently, it has become, in our collective imagination, a sea of precarious boats with a cargo filled with despair—boats overflowing with men, women, and children who brave shipwreck in order to reach the promised land. That sea, whose depths have yielded finds of immeasurable archaeological value, has today been transformed into a "marine cemetery"[3] of nameless dead. Now, more than ever, "the Mediterranean is a vast archive, an immense grave."[4]

We must rethink the Mediterranean, trying to geophilosophically scan the intricate web of issues that are tangled and intertwined in this name, which is replete with geohistorical and geosymbolic meanings. Thus we can perhaps demonstrate its complexity and envision a possible future for this sea, which is tied to its noble and glorious past but now runs the risk of becoming a tourism museum or a sacred place in our historical memories. If we reduce the Mediterranean to a mere archaeological excavation, looking for a lost past, which often borders on myth, we risk focusing simply on the precious but merely antiquarian history of its lost magnificence. As Predrag Matvejević correctly recognizes,

> Seeing the Mediterranean based only on its past is still a persistent habit. [. . .] The "patria of the myths" has been forced to suffer because of the mythologies that it has itself engendered or that others have contributed to nourishing. This space rich in history has been the victim of historicisms. There is still a tendency to confuse

A Sea That Unites and Divides

representation of reality with reality itself; the image of the Mediterranean and the real Mediterranean do not identify with each other at all. When it is broadened, an identity of being eclipses or rejects a poorly defined identity of doing. The retrospective continues to impose itself on the perspective. And, consequently, thought itself continues to be a prisoner of stereotypes.[5]

Some discussions about the Mediterranean have done nothing but feed stereotypes and clichés, which are difficult to get rid of. Such pompous discussions often feed into the worst demagogy, indifferently inciting to war or to peace, rekindling the flames of the most exacerbated nationalism or envisaging paradisiacal forms of civil coexistence among peoples.[6]

For all these reasons, it seems more prudent to steer clear of idyllic and oleographic images, as well as those drawn in gloomy hues. Both oversimplify the complexity that characterizes this particular geohistorical interweaving that we call the "Mediterranean."

Despite its apparent simplicity, it seems to me that the definition of Ferhat Horchani—one of many that I might have chosen—effectively summarizes the most salient features of this sea: "The Mediterranean can be defined with relative ease. It is a semi-closed sea on whose shores live very different peoples, who are nevertheless, very similar. It is a sea in the middle of lands and it is dominated by them, a sea in which peoples, due to their geographical position, are condemned to live together, to encounter the same problems, to have the same fears and to have the same hopes."[7] As an inland sea that is everywhere surrounded by lands, its unique character stems from the fact that it is overlooked by different civilizations and peoples, forced to share this space that is so easy to cross. At the same time, this sea unites these people, shaping them with common traits, and divides them, to the point that it produces irreconcilable conflicts. For this reason, "the Mediterranean is a unique place on our planet: cradle of civilization, land of gods, garden of Eden for some. In short, a sea that unites and divides."[8]

38   GEOPHILOSOPHY OF THE MEDITERRANEAN

Umbilicus Mundi, the Navel of the World

The uniqueness of the Mediterranean and its composite structure did not escape the geophilosophical interests of Hegel, who was inspired by the work of the geographer Carl Ritter entitled *Die Erdkunde im Verhältniß zur Natur und zur Geschichte des Menschen, oder allgemeine, vergleichende Geographie [. . .]*. Ritter had been Hegel's colleague in Berlin starting in 1820, and Hegel certainly drew inspiration from Ritter's work, which shaped his ideas about the geographical roots of the history of people.[9]

In his *Lectures on the Philosophy of History*, Hegel states that the most important geographical component in the historical development of a civilization is the relation between land and sea: "In the sphere of natural determinateness, the universal relation which is of most importance to history is that of *land and sea*."[10] Far from being something that facilitates separation, Hegel suggests that the watery space instead functions as a unifier: "We have become accustomed to look on water as a creator of divisions. The main objection to this is that nothing unites so effectively as water, for the civilized countries are invariably river territories. Water is in fact the uniting element, and it is the mountains which create divisions."[11] As a result, coastal areas are of particular importance as they clearly demonstrate how an immediate relationship with the sea usually induces the people who live there to be more open to exchanges and communication.

Moving from these two elements, the land and the sea, Hegel organizes a geography of the spirit, which allows him to distinguish between land and continental civilizations, such as the Asian ones, which are characterized by a strong and atavistic immobilism, and civilizations like the European one, which are instead extraordinarily dynamic precisely because of their relationship with the sea. In fact, the sea entails a specific form of existence, one that is forged in close contact with this moving element that is intolerant of any stable boundary. It encourages people to take risks and face danger, to go past every boundary, even risking their lives.[12] This idea of going beyond (which will be extensively explored by Nietzsche and his "aeronauts of the spirit")[13] appears in the thinking of Hegel as the very essence of the West, namely, of its innate *curiositas* and its restless and insatiable questioning. It goes so far as to risk shipwreck in its attempt to cross the Pillars of Hercules, where the extreme limit of a sea between lands opens up to the infinite space of the ocean.

It is precisely because it is treacherous that the sea forces people to be cunning. It is precisely because it is an element that appears "to adapt itself to all possible forms"[14] that it provokes thought to deal with it in various ways, experimenting with new technologies to tame it. This is the meaning of a passage from paragraph 247 of Hegel's *Elements of the Philosophy of Right*, a work that is so important for Carl Schmitt's thalassic thinking: "Just as the earth, the firm and *solid ground*, is a precondition of the principle of family life, so is the *sea* the natural element for industry, whose relations with the external world it enlivens."[15] For Hegel, as for Schmitt, marine and land existences are opposed to each other like a ship and a house. The latter adheres to the ground and is the symbol of stability, while the ship is the symbol of "the unstable depths,"[16] of becoming, and of an unstoppable fluctuation. While the first affirms an immutable eternity, the second, by contrast, alludes to the movement that characterizes both time and history. There is no doubt that Hegel prefers to live on the ship rather than in the house. He feels profoundly a part of that freedom from all constraints on which every *moving further* depends.

But what happens when the sea meets the earth, when land and sea, beyond their elementary opposition, are forced into a close confrontation, almost a close contact, as happens along the coasts of the Mediterranean?

For Hegel, the Old World, made up of the three great continental blocs of Africa, Asia, and Europe, revolves around a common fulcrum—the Mediterranean. They each overlook this sea, from which the entire history of the world unfolds:

> The Old World consists of three parts. [. . .] Their distinguishing feature is that they all lie around a sea

40 GEOPHILOSOPHY OF THE MEDITERRANEAN

which provides them with a focus and a means of communication. This is an extremely important factor. For the connecting link between these three continents, the *Mediterranean*, is the focus of the whole of world history. With its many inlets, it is not an ocean which stretches out indefinitely and to which man has a purely negative relationship; on the contrary, it positively invites him to venture out upon it. The Mediterranean Sea is the axis of world history. All the great states of ancient history lie around it, and it is the navel of the earth. Greece, that resplendent light of history, lies there. Then in Syria, Jerusalem is the centre of Judaism and Christianity; south-east of it lie Mecca and Medina, the fountainhead of the Moslem faith; to the west lie Delphi and Athens, with Rome and Carthage further west still; and to the south lies Alexandria, an even greater centre than Constantinople in which the spiritual fusion of east and west took place. The Mediterranean is therefore the heart of the Old World, its conditioning and vitalising principle. It is the centre of world history, in so far as the latter possesses any internal coherence. World history would be inconceivable without it; [. . .] for ancient history was strictly confined to the countries around the Mediterranean. [. . .] The latter is a major natural feature, and its influence is truly considerable; we cannot conceive of the historical process without the central and unifying element of the sea.[17]

Hegel even goes so far as to reason that the North African coasts, because they are projected onto the Mediterranean and separated by the desert from the rest of the African continent, should be fully incorporated into Europe.[18]

According to Hegel's geophilosophical interpretation, the Mediterranean therefore not only is the connecting fabric that holds together the three continents that overlook it but also becomes their center of gravity. It is the *umbilicus mundi*, the navel of the world, the beating heart from which the entire history of the world unfolds. As a point of connection between East and West, it is the birthplace of philosophy as well as of the three religions that derive from scriptures. The Mediterranean is not only a geographical entity but reveals itself as a space whose influence on the history of the world has been truly decisive.

However, Hegel does not hide the fact that the centrality of the Mediterranean is destined to wane. The discovery of the New World and, in particular, the affirmation of the North American continent have caused a real "spatial revolution"—as Schmitt sees it—which has shifted the focus of history toward America. Although America is still young and still developing, it announces itself as "the country of the future."[19] In the future, it is destined to overthrow the European hegemony of the Old World and the Mediterranean, which, as its internal sea, has determined its history in favor of the Atlantic, which is an *unlimited* oceanic expanse. It is from here that America, the daughter of the English thalassic empire, will impose its dominion over the world.

When Schmitt explored the irreversible crisis of the *jus publicum europaeum*, the European public law,[20] as the first truly *global* interstate law—which had guaranteed the centrality of Europe since the discovery of the New World—the Hegelian "prophecy" had been completely fulfilled. The new Atlantic power had already begun to show how much the Mediterranean was now only a sea of the "past." Hegel therefore grasps very sharply the importance of the Mediterranean for the ancient world as well as the causes of its inevitable decline once a new Atlantic power begins to dominate.

The Mediterranean, as its name suggests, is "a sea surrounded by land or a land touched by a sea."[21] It is the sea of the travels of Ulysses, the Homeric hero who most of all embodies the Mediterranean spirit and its versatile and moderate rationality, which is exposed to the limit in the incessant confrontation of land and sea.[22] But the Mediterranean is also the sea of Paul of Tarsus's missionary journeys. A Jew from the Diaspora, Paul was an indefatigable traveler along Mediterranean paths.[23] He went beyond the borders of the Jewish "enclosure" to spread throughout the entire Mediterranean the gospel of a universal salvation, which did not consider differences or "elections." At the boundary between two worlds (Judaism and Hellenism, East and West) and at the crossroads of many languages (he knew the Greek of the written and spoken word, the Hebrew of the sacred word, the Aramaic of Jesus and his first followers, and the Latin of the Roman Empire), Paul pushed himself to reach the most important Mediterranean ports and disembarked on its islands. He traversed its shores and stopped in its most important cities (Tarsus, Antioch, Jerusalem, Philippi, Thessalonica, Athens, Corinth, Ephesus, Rome), spreading a new creed of *universal* significance.

It is difficult to underestimate the value of this sea, which was the cradle of Europe and Western civilization. On its shores Athenian philosophy and democracy were born. It is in the Mediterranean that Roman law was disseminated and the three monotheistic religions of Arab Muslim, Christian, and Jewish worlds collide. Claiming the *Mediterranean* matrix of Europe means recognizing the complex articulation that first shaped and characterizes the West. It does not simply include the Judeo-Christian or Greek-Roman heritage but also fully involves the Arab Islamic tradition. It is this plurality of roots that is the most striking difference between the Old West (Europe and the great Mediterranean area) and the New West (the great area of North America).

There is no doubt that, as Hegel had foreseen, the affirmation of American oceanic power strips the Mediterranean of its centrality. The Mediterranean also runs the risk, though, of being relegated to a peripheral and completely negligible place compared to the new dynamics of globalization. Europe has forgotten its Mediterranean origins and now appears to be increasingly seduced by the call of an ocean that it was the first to cut a groove through when tracing new routes that were initially opened by the audacity of pirates and whalers. If Europe is to avoid its likely inevitable demise, it needs to urgently rethink the Mediterranean that was the lifeblood of its history and its roots. It must not, however, let itself be entangled in the nostalgic revisitation of its extraordinary past. Rather, it must respond in a new way, once again, to the challenge that the

A Sea That Unites and Divides   43

Old World threw down to itself by discovering the New World. Danilo Zolo is therefore right to say: "The key question is: Has the 'midland sea' really won the oceanic challenge by Christopher Columbus and Vasco de Gama?"[24]

A Sea of Differences

Trying to truly understand the status of the Mediterranean means, first of all, avoiding the risk of both an essentialist reductionism and a relativistic historicism. The Mediterranean does not represent an unchangeable essence and cannot be understood simply in terms of *one* immutable culture. Nor can it simply be reduced to an account of the history of the peoples who have dominated its shores over the centuries. If it is true that the Mediterranean defies any exhaustive definition, it is equally true that the multiplicity of differences that make it up must be understood in terms of their relationship to one another, not simply in terms of their historical succession. The Mediterranean is singular-plural; it is the extraordinary *relationship* between these differences, the meeting and the clash between different worlds, civilizations, religions, and languages that cannot be reduced to *one* entity. All of them have nevertheless managed to coexist, giving rise to a historical sedimentation with complex stratifications. Fernand Braudel has grasped better than anyone the intrinsically plural character of this singular space:

> What is the Mediterranean? A thousand things at once. Not one landscape, but landscapes without number. Not one sea, but a succession of seas. Not one civilization, but a number of civilizations, superimposed one on top of the other. To travel in the Mediterranean region is to find the Roman world in Lebanon, prehistory in Sardinia, Greek cities in Sicily, the Arab presence in Spain, and Turkish Islam in Yugoslavia. It is to reach far back in time, to the megalithic buildings of Malta

44   GEOPHILOSOPHY OF THE MEDITERRANEAN

> and the pyramids of Egypt. [. . .] All this is because the
> Mediterranean is a very ancient crossroads on which, for
> thousands of years, everything has converged: men, beasts
> of burden, vehicles, merchandise, ships, ideas, religions,
> and the arts of living. Even plants.[25]

The Mediterranean is not a single civilization, but a melting pot of different cultures. Its very geomorphology reflects the intricate complication of elements that compose it:

> The Mediterranean is not even a *single* sea, it is a com-
> plex of seas; and these seas are broken up by islands,
> interrupted by peninsulas, ringed by intricate coastlines.
> Its life is linked to the land, its poetry more than half-ru-
> ral, its sailors may turn peasant with the seasons; it is
> the sea of vineyards [. . .] and its history can no more
> be separated from that of the lands surrounding it than
> the clay can be separated from the hands of the potter
> who shapes it.[26]

Even today, according to Braudel, there are three great civilizations that make up the whole, with their particular styles of life, of thought, of religious beliefs, "three monsters always ready to show their teeth, three characters with interminable destinies, ever present, at least for centuries and centuries."[27] The first is the European West, which was created on the basis of Judeo-Christian and Roman heritage; the second, the Islamic world, asserts itself *against* the first as an enemy and complementary brother. The hostility and rivalry between the two also reveal the mimetic nature of a relationship that has experienced moments of profound osmosis. Finally, there is the Orthodox world, which stretches from Greece to Russia and whose fault lines cross the Balkans, causing frequent earthquakes that have always made that area unstable.

It is clear that the difficult coexistence between its different souls is the source of widespread conflicts that have always characterized the Mediterranean area. The situation has been correctly discerned by Matvejević, who effaces any idealized image of the

Mediterranean: "Nations and races have conjoined and disjoined here over the centuries; more peoples have lived with one another and clashed with one another here than perhaps anywhere on the planet. Overplaying their similarities and interchanges and underplaying their differences and conflicts is so much bravado."[28] Therefore, we should not underestimate the conflictual nature of the Mediterranean: from the very beginning, its shores have witnessed the clash of civilizations. As Braudel wrote: "Civilizations are therefore steeped in war and hatred, an immense grey area that almost devours them in half. They create hate, they feed on it, they live on it. . . . Too often, indeed, civilizations exist with nothing but misunderstanding, scorn, and loathing for the other."[29] Currently, the Israeli-Palestinian conflict, which is the most painful and almost incurable wound in the Mediterranean, is symbolically like a fracture that divides the world into two opposing blocs. How can we deny that, in the Mediterranean, it appears as an incurable plague that blatantly impedes any attempt at pacification?[30]

Yet the clash is not the fatal outcome of the confrontation between civilizations, even though they are jealous guardians of their own individuality. If, from time to time, the Mediterranean has known dominant civilizations, none, however, in the end, has ever been able to cancel its competitors. Rather, each civilization had to graft itself onto the others. They are stratifications whose sediment is visible not as a foreign body but, rather, as a tangible trace of its own passage, which has come to incorporate itself, to add to the others, enriching the set of new elements. From one coast to another, exchanges, dialogue, and contacts have multiplied, generating fruitful contaminations, which have given rise to a common history: "If, to the civilizations on its shores, the sea owes the wars that disrupted its waters, it also owes them the multiplicity of exchanges (technologies, ideas, and even beliefs), as well as the multi-colored heterogeneity of the sights it offers our eyes today. The Mediterranean is a mosaic of all the existing colors."[31]

One and many, the Mediterranean is a polychrome and polyphonic whole that has always been resistant to any *reductio ad unum*. As Matvejević rightly points out:

46 GEOPHILOSOPHY OF THE MEDITERRANEAN

> There is no single Mediterranean culture; rather there is a Mediterranean with many cultures. Cultures characterized by some quite similar features and by others which are very different. The similarities are motivated by the proximity of a common sea and by the meeting on its shores of nations and forms of expression very close to each other. And the differences are marked by reasons of origin and history, as well as of beliefs and customs. However, neither the similarities nor the differences are absolute or constant; rather the first sometimes prevail and, at other times, the second.[32]

For this reason, the obvious differences and numerous divisions have not yet managed to tear those underground ties that continue to keep the Mediterranean peoples together, even beyond their apparent opposition.[33] When it does not take the form of an irremediable conflict, the confrontation with otherness, the close encounter with the other can in fact be the lifeblood that every culture needs to nourish itself, if it is not to be stifled. Otherwise, it will close in on itself in a paranoid defense to the bitter end of the uncontaminated "purity" of its identity.[34]

It is only by taking a broader view that we can grasp the tiles of a mosaic in this sea of differences. It is only by stepping back that the overall design finally becomes visible. It thus becomes possible to understand what Braudel called the "profound essence of the Mediterranean," its "original unity."[35] It is a unity that is itself multiple,[36] plural, but not any less singular. It is here that different identities can coexist if each agrees not to dominate the other and instead agrees to listen to one another. For this to happen—as it did in some happy moments of Mediterranean history[37]—it is necessary to rethink the very concept of border and frontier:[38] "Inhabiting the frontier therefore means being willing to cross borders, travelling across the border that separates one's own from the stranger, putting one's own identity into play, redefining it in comparison with the identities of others, and discovering that each of us hosts innumerable doubles."[39] Not an insurmountable

A Sea That Unites and Divides 47

demarcation line, which defines a closed and excluding identity space—and, precisely for this reason, is always on the verge of transforming confrontation into a clash and the frontier into a war front—"the border is the place where two differences come into contact and they each discover, through the other, their narrowness."[40] It is only by probing borders that we are able to articulate a confrontation that does not result in nihilistic relativism or in a mere test of strength but allows differences to exist *together* without pretending to incorporate or annihilate the other. The Mediterranean was—and therefore could still be—the experience of this sharing, of this relationship that simultaneously maintains relationships while safeguarding distance and differences.

The Mediterranean Pluriverse

As we have seen, the Mediterranean is a sea that is rich in coasts and shores, peninsulas and islands; it is a sea that separates and divides but, above all, connects from one port to another. Here, borders multiply along lines of constant tension that have often transformed the Mediterranean into a sea of war, clashes, and blood. Nevertheless, this plurality of borders makes the Mediterranean not only a site of clashes but, equally, a place of endless engagement with the other, preventing any drastic *reductio ad unum*. If we are to avoid a purely nostalgic or regressive return to its myths, it is because the Mediterranean is not simply a sea of the past but could still have a future. Without doubt, "an essential condition for this to happen is to rethink the relationship between the process of unification of Europe, its belonging to the Western Hemisphere, its Mediterranean roots, and its relationship with the Islamic world."[41] Europe must recognize the Mediterranean as its cradle and turn back toward its shores, which have for too long been forgotten at its peripheral edges. Only then can Europe truly rediscover its "natural" (from a geohistorical point of view) focal point. It must not look to this sea with nostalgic regret for its lost importance in the history of the world. Instead, it should adopt a

48 GEOPHILOSOPHY OF THE MEDITERRANEAN

proud awareness of constituting a "large space" capable of neutralizing conflicts and avoiding the dangers of a clash of civilizations. By becoming a place of dialogue and meeting, the Mediterranean "could transform itself into place of peace between the West and the Islamic world and play an important role in launching a peace process on a global scale."[42]

Its indelible plurality could function as an exemplary paradigm in the era of globalization precisely because it demonstrates how unity and differences, pluralism and universalism, far from opposing each other and pushing in different directions, can coexist and articulate themselves in the same wide area. The Mediterranean can truly constitute an *alternative*[43] to the neoimperial design of a new world order, whichever side it comes from. It could counterpoise any abstract, ideological, and homologating universalism and demonstrate the need for a pluriverse that would even include Islam, that absolute Enemy, and the Arab world as integral parts.[44]

The *pluralistic universalism*[45] of the Mediterranean derives from the continuing peaceful or conflictual interaction between different languages, customs, habits, traditions. Unlike Atlantic monistic universalism, it therefore presents an opportunity to rethink the entire global order. While the Atlantic "one mindedness or single thought [*pensiero unico*]" is allergic to any cultural and religious difference and uses the universalism of human rights as a pretext to wage humanitarian wars, the plural universe of the Mediterranean does not erase the differences. Instead, it must be able to combine unity and multiplicity while avoiding any fundamentalism. As Cassano writes: "The adjective *Mediterranean* contains a cultural and political program, because it describes a sea that unites and divides, that lies *between* lands without belonging exclusively to any of them, that is allergic to all fundamentalisms."[46] The *Mare nostrum* is a common sea that no one has ever been able to appropriate or monopolize. It is precisely for this reason that it might be capable of providing a space of inclusion rather than exclusion and integration rather than fundamentalism. If fundamentalism is ultimately a rejection of the otherness of the other as well as an overbearing desire to impose the dominion of the One and the Same on the

A Sea That Unites and Divides 49

reality of the many and the different, then the Mediterranean is the geophilosophical place where this hubris shows all its violent senselessness. Here, the sea, as the Limitless, constantly collides with the land, which holds it in check and gives it measure, while the land cannot delude itself into dictating its absolute law, its immobility, but must come to terms with the mobility of the sea. The latter flows along the coasts, incessantly disturbing the land, cracking its stability, eroding and fraying its profile, and forcing it to move. The island,[47] which is a land that seems to float on the surface of the water, is therefore the most fitting symbol of the interpenetration between land and sea; the archipelago is therefore the geophilosophical symbol of the Mediterranean.

As a sea *between* lands, the Mediterranean is therefore the place par excellence of relationship, interrelationship, incessant questioning, and the continuous exchange of the self with the stranger. It is a place of interminable translation. Although it is important to emphasize the need for dialogue between the different languages, cultures, and religions that make up the Mediterranean pluriverse, this dialogic paradigm runs the risk of slipping into an irenicism, a peacefulness that is too easily denied by the objective difficulties of understanding each other. It runs the risk of forgetting too quickly and underestimating those differences that must be valued since they only produce the richness of a world where *different* voices can harmonize in a polyphonic song. The Mediterranean "harmony" can only arise from the conflict of interpretations and the patient work of *translation*[48] of one language into another. Translation, in fact, is the experience not only of encounter and exchange between the self and the stranger but also of a difference and distance that can never be completely erased. In fact, there is no translation without a *remainder* of untranslatability; the confrontation with the stranger is never completely resolved and dissolved in the self and in a totally complete appropriation. Unlike dialogue, translation emphasizes the irreducible extraneousness and the difference that remains at the heart of every possible understanding. Moreover, translation denounces the Babelic origin of languages and the arrogance that would attempt to reduce them to only *one*. It

50   GEOPHILOSOPHY OF THE MEDITERRANEAN

demonstrates both that we cannot appropriate the other's language and that the language that we speak—that is, *our* language—is, in turn, never entirely suitable and can never be completely "proper." An idiom is never pure; we always speak in the language of the other. We are always in translation, even when we think we are speaking in our own language. There is nothing other than translation at the origin of language, and indeed of every language, in its relationship with itself and with others, since they feed on their own differing, that is, on the extraneousness that constitutes their secret and inviolable heart. The Mediterranean has always been a sea of mandatory and impossible translations, starting from the prodigious work of the Seventy, who translated the Hebrew Bible into the Greek language of nascent Christianity, which would later assume Latin as its *universal* language. But it was also the place where the Arab language and culture met and were translated on the many other shores of this sea, leaving indelible traces, as is apparent in toponymy and numerous dialects.

But translating does not only mean establishing a dialogue that respects the irreducibility of the differences between languages, inside and outside of them. It also means *hosting* the language of the other, welcoming it as a *stranger*. In the ports of the Mediterranean, ships have found refuge, as have the languages that have landed on shore. They have contaminated the coasts, settled on the shores, undermined any appropriation and any attempt to fence them in. From shore to shore, from the Greek world to the Latin one and in all three religions of the Book, the unreserved hospitality, which recognizes the stranger as a *sacred* guest, constitutes the real cultural horizon[49] of the Mediterranean that is today shamefully forgotten.

Even if the scenarios that we have before our eyes seem daunting, I must agree with those who believe that "another Mediterranean is possible"[50] and that, indeed, "the Mediterranean can be thought of as a possible 'alternative.'"[51]

Provided that the Mediterranean is able to think of itself as a "plural universe" that does not deny differences, it can become the driving force of a new nomos, a new law of the earth that constitutes itself as a pluriverse—free from hostility and the clash of civilizations and, instead, characterized by hospitality and translation.

Four

Cartographies of Italy

A Greeting Card

As part of his 2010 Christmas celebrations, Roberto Calderoli, the Northern League minister at the time, decided to send a special Christmas card. At the top was an inscription that read: "We are turning the country upside down—Ministries out of Rome!" Another inscription at the bottom bore good news: "Federalism—Dreams become reality." The image on the Christmas card was unsettling in many ways. It featured an upside-down Italy transformed into a Christmas tree, complete with colored balls and a Christmas comet at the top, placed between Scylla and Charybdis (see figure 4.1). The full meaning of this whimsical representation and the accompanying inscriptions is clear from the monochromatic green Christmas ornaments that are scattered all over the map. Inside these decorations is the symbol of the Northern League. The politicians of the Northern League have overlooked the early meaning of this symbol, which was originally related to the sun, much like the swastika. They renamed it the "Sun of the Alps." Even the comet is represented by this symbol, which bears a "tail." The overall meaning is quite obvious and it is indeed oversimplified by the iconographic language of our former "Minister for Simplification."

Figure 4.1. The Northern League's upside-down Italy. Public domain.

We could read the card in the following way: we are reversing the politics of this country; we are even flipping and overturning the inveterate logic of power, which has always looked to Rome as *caput mundi*, as the center of the world, and has sacrificed the development of the North to the inertia of the South, dwindling its enormous resources by supporting it. The Northern League's picture of Italy, in fact, deforms its cartographic reality. It clearly demonstrates that a geographic map cannot be reduced to a simple geophysical survey; a map also reveals the world as seen by the person who traces its outlines.[1] Much like medieval cartography, the Northern League's map represents a spiritual geography that is so powerful as to deform the edges of the familiar boot shape (that is, the geographical image usually associated with the Italian peninsula). Here, in fact, Italy appears much wider in its base; it is a clear sign of a booming "Padania" (that is, the area surrounding the Po River)—to use the geographical and geopolitical term coined by Northern League—while the rest of Italy is decidedly shorter and less slender than normal. It is clear that the southern areas have been shrunk and sacrificed, as a sign of their insignificance. The geopolitical indications scattered about the map are even more revealing. In the first place, they show a real *translatio imperii*, a transfer of rules by means of the massive displacement of the ministries out of Rome, where only those of Foreign Affairs and Justice are left. It is perhaps a consolatory acknowledgment of the past, when Rome was the capital of the empire, whose borders enclosed much of the then-known world, as well as the birthplace of law. Yet this is just precisely that, a blurred memory. The ministries that "matter" and, above all, the CONSOB (Commissione Nazionale per le Società e la Borsa) and the federal senate (the beating heart of federal power) are firmly established in Padania in this image. Here, the Sun of the Alps balls multiply and shimmer with their very green light. Down at the bottom of the boot, we find instead the Ministries of the Environment and Health in Campania, plagued by waste (from the North), and the Ministry of Internal Affairs in Calabria, to counter the 'Ndrangheta, the Mafia, and the Camorra, which are notoriously confined to those territories. The Ministry of Tourism is obviously placed in Sardinia, whose tourist vocation has always been very close to the heart of our former head of government, Silvio Berlusconi, who owns lots of houses there. Finally, Sicily, considered to be strategically placed *against* the Mediterranean, is rightfully entitled to the Ministry of Defense, in order to adequately counter the new "barbaric invasions" of migrants from the other shore.

What is the geophilosophy[2] of this map of Italy? What message did it try to convey to a country that was preparing to celebrate its 150 years? Despite its apparent playfulness, this upside-down map of Italy marks the beginning of a new "ideological" cartography. The green of the boot, where the Po Valley ministries seem even greener, does not hide the ambition to "colonize" the entire peninsula and its islands, as if only Northern League federalism might create a new identity for the country in the sign of the Sun of the Alps. This upside-down Italy stands out against the blue of a *shoreless* sea. Enlarged in its continental part, it is pompously swollen and bellied due to its great binge on ministries. This version of Italy sees nothing on the horizon, especially not the North African coasts that are so close to Sicily. An invisible boundary

54 GEOPHILOSOPHY OF THE MEDITERRANEAN

seems to surround it on all sides, like a fortress that is deluded enough to thinks itself impregnable. The Mediterranean sun has been replaced with the Sun of the Alps, which shines like a comet on the Strait of Messina, where the Northern League dreams of building a gigantic bridge. It is an illusion that tries to seduce a place that wishes to remain an island. In fact, those who live along the seacoasts know perfectly well that the sea itself is a "bridge" that not only separates but also unites. It has always connected and facilitated communication, without the need for any grandiose buildings in concrete and steel. But the Northern League seems to ignore this, as well as the fact that even the densest mountain range hides many passes and passages; the history of the Alps is made of intense exchanges that occur between one slope and another.

Tabula Rogeriana

Calderoli's "gimmick" of turning Italy upside down is not all that original, although he probably does not realize it. In fact, the orientation of maps does not always place the north at the top. For example, the famous Ebstorf *Mappa mundi* (1239)—which survived for over seven centuries and was unfortunately destroyed during World War II bombings—is oriented to the east, indicated by the effigy of Christ at the top. At the center, the city of Jerusalem is situated as the symbolic *umbilicus mundi*, the world's navel (see figure 4.2).

The inverted orientation of the Northern League's Italy has a precedent that is even more famous, though probably unknown to the minister. I refer to the extraordinary tables of a renowned medieval geographer, who gifted us the most faithful cartographic representation of the world at his time.

His full name is long and perhaps too complicated for a former Minister of Simplification. Moreover, it is an Arabic name—surely an aggravating factor that would make it even more suspicious in

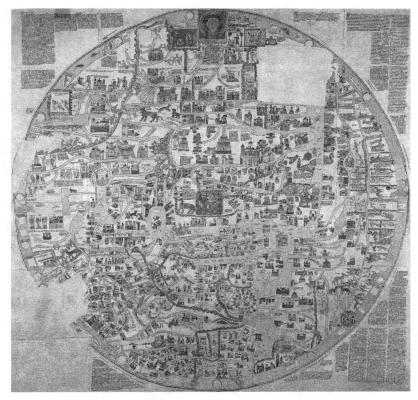

Figure 4.2. Ebstorf *Mappa mundi*. Public domain.

his eyes: Abu Abd Allah Muhammad ibn Muhammad ibn Abd Allah ibn Idris al Siqilli. We could simplify it, in the spirit of the former minister, and refer to him as Idrisi, "the Sicilian." His name is closely linked to that of Roger II of Hauteville, who was crowned in Palermo as Norman king of Sicily on Christmas night, 1130, with a sumptuous ceremony. The memory of that night is preserved forever in a stunning mosaic in the church of the Martorana in Palermo. It shows Christ himself placing the crown on Roger's head.[3] The Norman king had succeeded in consolidating his power in Sicily and had also successfully reunified the various

Norman regions of southern Italy into one single kingdom. By the time he died in 1154, the Kingdom of Sicily was at the height of its power and splendor and extended as far north as Pescara. The secret of this extensive territorial power lay in Roger's conception of government. Raised in the cosmopolitan environment of the Palermo court and educated by Greek and Muslim tutors, Roger spoke Greek, Arabic, and Latin, as well as Sicilian. During his reign, Sicily enjoyed a period of maximum splendor. In many ways, it paved the way for the cosmopolitan and universalistic spirit of the worthiest of Roger's successors, Frederick II of Swabia, the *Stupor mundi*, who was born of the marriage between Roger's daughter, Constance of Hauteville, and Emperor Henry VI of Swabia.

Roger was a man of vast culture, but, above all, he was curious and open to all types of knowledge. He loved the pomp and splendor that was typical of oriental courts, and he was able to translate this opulence into an extraordinary drive to the sciences and the arts. Under his reign, the Palatine Chapel and the Church of the Martorana were built in Palermo, with their splendid mosaics inspired by the Byzantine canon and the unique architecture characteristic of the Arab-Norman style. He also oversaw the building of San Giovanni degli Eremiti, which is one of the most striking examples of this style, complete with red domes. Even the splendid Cathedral of Cefalù was built by Roger. It was perhaps intended as a thankful votive offering for his narrow escape from shipwreck and his unexpected salvation as his boat managed to dock at Cefalù.

There was a large Muslim and Jewish population in Palermo under Roger's rule, even though he was a Christian king. Even the more ancient Byzantine populations found acceptance and tolerance. Roger's Sicily was, as never before, at the heart of the Mediterranean, enjoying intense commercial as well as cultural exchange along all of its shores. It was a luxuriant and fertile land, by virtue of innovative agricultural and irrigation techniques that the Arabs had imported. The palaces were of unparalleled magnificence, and Sicily was a beacon of science, arts, and culture for the whole of medieval Europe.

It is in this cosmopolitan context that Roger, driven by a desire to learn more about the world around him, invited the greatest geographer of the time to live at his court. Idrisi arrived in Palermo around 1145 and remained there until his death, about 1164. Probably a native of Ceuta, in present-day Morocco, Idrisi not only was the most talented geographer of the time but was also renowned for his botanical skills, especially in the field of medicinal plants. He collected a large number of specimens and was always attentive to their therapeutic properties. Roger closely followed the developments of Idrisi's tireless research as he devoted himself to mapping out the entire known world. This exceptional and laborious work resulted in the creation of a planisphere that was engraved from his meticulous cartographic drawings. It was etched on a silver plate that weighed 150 kilograms. Its diameter stretched almost two meters. The plate was made for the king to see shortly before his death in 1154. Unfortunately, the work had a short life, as it was looted and melted down in 1161 during a revolt. But we are left with other very important testimonies to Idrisi's cartographic production, such as a geographical text known as *Al-Kitab al-Rujari* (*The Book of Roger*).[4] Roger himself referred to it as *The Excursion of One Eager to Penetrate the Horizons* (*Nuzhat al-mushtāq fī ikhtirāq al-āfāq*). It attests to a truly extraordinary geographical knowledge for the time, which was the result of Idrisi's numerous journeys as well as the stories of the numerous travelers who passed through Sicily and were interviewed at length. It is the culmination of meticulous and patient research that lasted over fifteen years. What is most striking in reading *Nuzhat al-mushtāq* is the extreme precision and conciseness of the descriptions, which are of a wholly realistic and "scientific" nature, conceding little or nothing to fiction.

Some important remnants of Idrisi's cartography still exist, including a circular map (a three-meter reproduction was on show at the exhibition *1001 Inventions: Discover the Muslim Heritage in Our World* at the London Science Museum, February–June 2010; see figure 4.3). There is also a rectangular map of the world called *Tabula Rogeriana* (see figure 4.4). Its profoundly innovative character

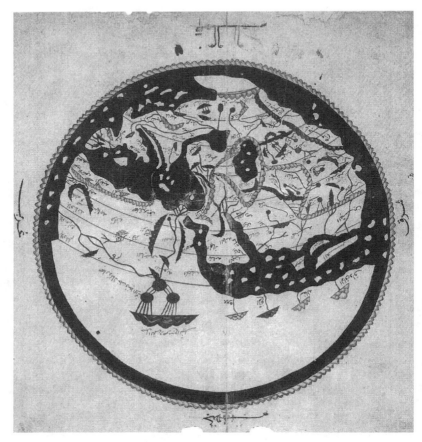

Figure 4.3. Al-Idrisi's circular world map. Public domain.

is immediately apparent. While preserving certain elements derived from the Ptolemaic tradition, Idrisi was able to free himself from such conventions. His free and profoundly revolutionary outlook meant that he was unwilling to let himself be bound by religious or theological demands. In this regard, he anticipates the scientific approach and spirit of observation that is typical of the modern age. If his work had not been forgotten for four centuries, cartographic knowledge would have developed at a much faster rate.

At first glance, these two maps allow us to grasp an interesting detail that relates back to the topics I considered at the beginning

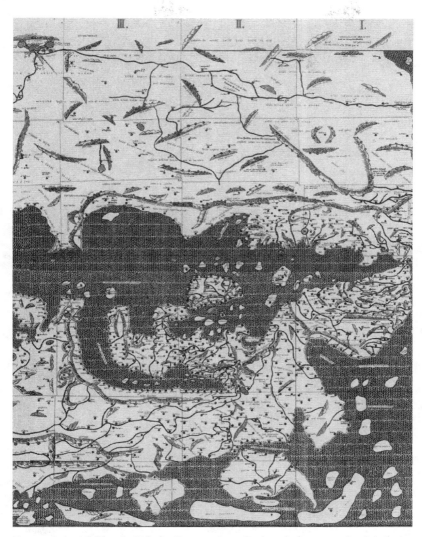

Figure 4.4. Al-Idrisi's *Tabula Rogeriana* with detail showing the Mediterranean. Public domain.

of my reflections: followings Arab customs, Idrisi orients the maps in the opposite way to ours—that is, he places the south above, in a similar fashion to the Northern League minister's Christmas card with Italy upside down, even though the minister was no doubt entirely unaware of this illustrious precedent.

When compared to the Ebstorf *Mappa mundi*, Idrisi's map shows a more compact world. It is extraordinary in the precision of its detail, even though it dates from almost a century earlier. No sacred symbols are present, and, above all, the Mediterranean basin and the coasts bordering it are portrayed with particular accuracy.

To appreciate the details even more, let us try to dissect the part that concerns Italy and explore the results of this comparison—in a slightly irreverent and provocative way. Compared to the upside-down Italy from which we started, the relationships of this other upside-down Italy seem absolutely inverted. In this case, the boot, although it is perfectly recognizable, seems to swell and expand in its final part, while the sea digs deeply into its profile, drawing wide gulfs and inlets (see figure 4.5).

Sicily seems incredibly large, and its archipelagos of islands seem to touch and almost merge with those of the Gulf of Naples. It is as if Idrisi's Italy entirely converged with the revered Roger II's Kingdom of Sicily, as if there were not much else beyond the Norman borders of his kingdom (see figure 4.6).

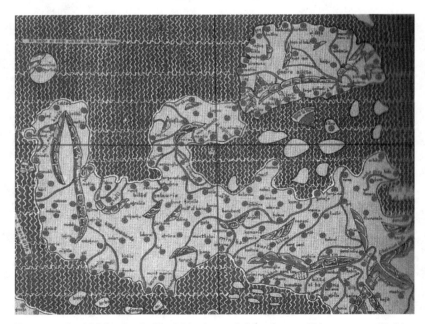

Figure 4.5. Al-Idrisi's *Gulf of Naples and Islands*, twelfth century. Public domain.

Figure 4.6. Al-Idrisi's *Sicily*, twelfth century. Public domain.

What geophilosophy emerges from Idrisi's maps? What can we learn from this upside-down proto-Italy, which is a jagged peninsula that extends into the Mediterranean, whose center is a magnified Sicily? The latter appears separated from the peninsula by a very thin strip of sea, just enough to guarantee its proud insularity. But it also binds it to the destiny of a kingdom that lasted, with ups and downs and different dynasties, from Roger II's *Regnum Siciliae* (1130) until 1816, when it was transformed into the Kingdom of the Two Sicilies, with practically unchanged territories until 1861—that is, until the unification of Italy.

Mediterranean Italy

The Normans, as the name itself indicates—Northmen or Norsemen, that is, men of the North—originally came from the deep north, from Scandinavia; therefore, they came from further north than Padania. Yet, like few, they were able to interpret and understand the profound cultures of the southern lands and peoples they had conquered. Roger II, the Norman, together with Frederick

II, the Swabian, testify to this aspect. Of course, the world represented by Idrisi's precious maps—that is, the world of his king Roger—has now irrevocably disappeared. No southern ideology, no Southern League could ever resurrect it. And yet, how can we deny that that world continues to secretly feed our dreams? This incurable nostalgia has nourished southern and Sicilian arrogance as well as a culture that has produced and continues to produce works of extraordinary value, especially in Sicily. It is our daily bread, our cross, and our delight: all that was once splendor and greatness now evokes a dark pain, a sense of irreversible defeat and lost prestige, as well as an acute sense of impotence, which often results in a widespread feeling of *cupio dissolvi*. To understand the "resentment" of the South, its ingrained resistance to what the North calls "development," one must first understand the history from which we came. This history, which I have succinctly narrated up to now, seems today largely forgotten, not only on the other side of Italy but even by those who now inhabit those same places that are scarred, mortified, and disfigured by those who should protect them.

Yet from Idrisi's extraordinarily vivid cartographic images can perhaps emerge valuable pointers for the future, beyond any nostalgia for the past. First of all, what clearly appears is the Mediterranean vocation of Italy, which overlooks that sea on at least three sides, as is masterfully illustrated by these maps. Of course, with the opening of oceanic routes, starting from the discovery of the New Continent, it has lost much of the centrality that once made it the *umbilicus mundi*. But how can we fail to see that the Mediterranean is still, in many ways, the crucial sea, at least for Europe? There lies its past and origin but also the means to map out its future.

Despite numerous doubts, crises, criticisms, and self-criticisms, it is only by starting from this sea and from this peninsula, which, more than any other, wedges its lands in it, that Europe could fully appreciate the significance of its multiple identity. It is by diving back into its waters that Europe could soothe the serious illness that grips its spirit. According to Husserl and Heidegger,

Europe has its birthplace in Greece and is identified with the very birth of philosophy. On the other hand, it is deeply rooted in Judeo-Christian—not only religious—traditions. But the Sicily of Roger and Idrisi also reminds us of the profound and decisive influence of Arab and Muslim culture, in all its expressive forms, which has penetrated and enlightened our history for centuries.

Even today, the Sicily of Roger II and his cartographer Idrisi continues to show the foresight of this perspective, of this view of the sea. Only the Mediterranean Italy of Idrisi could still recover its own vocation, inscribed in its geography, looking at that Sicily which, far from being a marginal place in history, became its theater when it was able to be not a frontier land, closed within its own miserable isolation, but a welcome space, a place of encounter and dialogue between languages, cultures, religions, knowledge. Sicily was able to peacefully bring together peoples, affiliations, faiths, and customs that were irreducible enemies elsewhere.

The process of unification of Italy—as is well known—began at the top. It is now a question of completing this process from the bottom up. The Sicily of Idrisi, whose maps were written in Arabic characters, challenges us to look toward the other side of the Mediterranean, beyond any anachronistic colonial temptation. The upheavals that cross it present a challenge and an appeal to our shared identity as inhabitants of the two shores of the same sea and require Europe to rediscover the place of its origin in order to resist, now more than ever, the Atlantic temptation. Only a Mediterranean Italy aware of its geographical and geopolitical position could be the go-between for this necessary European "conversion."

Returning to the Mediterranean, beyond any nostalgia or rhetoric, is also important for rethinking that convulsive reshuffling of borders and frontiers that accompanies the ongoing processes of global unification. At least in its best moment, it shows the possibility of a coexistence between differences that are not only irreducible but whose meeting and mixing (as opposed to indistinctness) have produced an extraordinary cultural and social richness.[5] In an era where a universalist perspective now appears

64 GEOPHILOSOPHY OF THE MEDITERRANEAN

to be an obligatory choice for human coexistence on this planet, the Mediterranean *pluriverse* offers itself as a paradigm of a unity that is respectful—indeed, proud—of the differences that compose it. At the same time, it can be an antidote to the centralizing and homogenizing effects of ongoing globalization.

What has recently been called the "Mediterranean alternative"[6] suggests a special *relationship* (which will be achievable in the future because it has already been realized in the past) between different worlds, civilizations, religions, and languages, which could never be reduced to one. In the Mediterranean, however, they have found forms of coexistence, giving rise to a historical layering with a complex stratification. It is not a single civilization but a melting pot of different cultures. It is a multiple, plural, but no less singular unity in itself, wherein different identities accept contamination and can coexist only if they do not attempt to dominate each other and, instead, they listen to one other. The Mediterranean has been the experience of this sharing, and it launches this challenge to the globalized world. It bears witness to how unity and differences, pluriverse and universe, far from opposing each other and pushing in different directions, can in fact coexist and articulate wide spaces in a way that is not necessarily in conflict. It is precisely for this reason that the Mediterranean can constitute an *alternative* to the neoimperial design of a new world order, from whatever side it comes. It can counteract false centralizing, ideological, and homogenizing universalism by demonstrating the need for a decentralized and truly anti-Ptolemaic pluriverse.

The *pluralistic universalism* of the Mediterranean, due to the continuous exchange and translation between different languages, customs, habits, and traditions, therefore constitutes, unlike any monistic universalism, a challenge to rethink the entire global order.

Currently, it is up to Italy to respond to this challenge; only Italy, above all other European countries, bears the indelible and tangible signs of the Mediterranean in its history and geography. It must listen and relaunch its deep vocation and its hidden sense of unity, which is also that of Europe. Almost a millennium ago, this had already been foreseen by the Arab Sicilian Idrisi, with his extraordinary cartographic feat at the court of the Norman king of Sicily, Roger II, in Palermo—a cosmopolitan city and an outpost, in the Mediterranean, of the whole ecumene.

Five

The Origin of Messina

Figure 5.1. Miniature of the city of Messina, artist unknown, from the poem "Rhegina" by Angelo Callimaco Siculo (National Library of Rome). Public domain.

68 GEOPHILOSOPHY OF THE MEDITERRANEAN

The Loss of Place

In his famous *Erörterung* of Georg Trakl's poetry, Heidegger recalls how the original meaning of *Ort*—the German word for "place"—refers to the tip of a spear (*die Spitze des Speers*): "All parts of the spear converge at the tip. The place [*Ort*] gathers unto itself, supremely and in the extreme. Its gathering power penetrates and pervades everything. The place, the gathering power, gathers in and preserves all it has gathered, not like an encapsulating shell but rather by penetrating with its light all it has gathered, and only thus releasing it into its own nature."[1] "Place" is that point of convergence, meeting, and recollection (*Versammlung*) where, much like in the sharp point of a spear, space concentrates itself by virtue of an irresistible attraction. As the center point[2] of an invisible cross, each Place is simultaneously an *umbilicus*, a navel, and an *Axis mundi*, a world axis, a point of conjunction between Heaven and Earth, or *Geviert* (Fourfold),[3] to use Heidegger's expression. It is the meeting point of the quadrature—that is, the crossroads between Heaven and Earth and between the divines and the mortals, insofar as it unfolds a space where humans can dwell.

The Place[4] thus guards and safeguards human dwelling on earth. It is not a coffin that keeps its precious contents closed within itself, making it in some way inaccessible. Rather, it illuminates dwelling and brings it into that light where everything is able to unfold its own essence. It is the Openness that every time and everywhere opens up a world and makes it a habitable space for humans. In the reciprocal communication between Heaven and Earth, between humans and the divines, it is at the crossroads of those directionalities that, in space-time, intersect and generate Places. It is the coming into the world of an Earth-under-Heaven where mortals are confined within the limits of each being, but, at the same time, they are turned to Heaven, toward a silent call coming from Elsewhere.

Are our cities Places? Do they really allow space and time to dwell? Are the disordered assemblages of buildings in the urban space still homes that are capable of protecting the *Geviert*, the

THE ORIGIN OF MESSINA 69

Fourfold? "The Place [*Ort*] is a shelter [*eine Hut*] for the fourfold [*Geviert*] or, by the same token, a house [*ein Huis, ein Haus*]."[5] Do Places still exist? Or, have they by now been taken over by non-places of the type described by Marc Augé,[6] including airports, large hotel complexes, shopping malls, and hypermarkets? These are all examples of a homologating globalization, which eliminates differences and erases the singularity of places.

The reasons for this creeping homologation are far reaching. Nietzsche was among the first to foresee and describe it appropriately as a "growing desert" that not only gradually dries the earth, reducing once fertile and cultivated lands into a uniform desert landscape, but also disallows any future growth. Nietzsche called this process, which prevents any rooting, "European nihilism" and saw it as "the uncanniest of all guests." He refers to it as the "deadly disease" that has been incubating on European soil for a long time to spread across the entire globe. It coincides with the westernization of the world that has now become reality. After Nietzsche, the word *nihilism* brings together the most acute analyses of the twentieth century, highlighting the most important aspects of the period, even though from different perspectives. Jünger explores the nihilism of the Worker as a servant of technology who uniformly shapes the world in the Worker's own image and likeness. The worker reduces everything to Work, quantity, and calculation, triggering powerful processes of global unification and uniformity, wherein every difference is destined to disappear. In this unstoppable march forward, everything turns into a tabula rasa. Heidegger, by contrast, describes nihilism as uprooting, or the loss of roots (*Entwurzelung*), as homelessness (*Heimatlosigkeit*), identifying it as the *Stimmung* of our time. Indeed, nihilism represents the internal logic of all Western thought, which only recently, and particularly starting with the modern age, finally becomes clear. But it is to Carl Schmitt that we owe the most detailed analysis of the historical processes that finally led to an inexorable *Ent-ortung*, an unprecedented de-localization. This de-localization inaugurated a *globale Zeit*, a global age in which the entire terrestrial globe, now fully encompassed in one overall gaze, resists any nomos that is

70 GEOPHILOSOPHY OF THE MEDITERRANEAN

capable of ordering it, like an immense expanse of ocean whose smooth, vast surface resembles a desert.[7]

The loss of the Place therefore occurs as part of a nihilistic process pertaining to the internal logic of the Western *ratio*, the rationality that has now become the dominant and *only* way of thinking on this terraqueous orb. Any attempt at re-localization will necessarily have to deal with this history—that is, with the destiny of the West that has become the entire world. We must not, therefore, succumb to the temptations of comfortable nostalgia. Rather, we must go *beyond* the unavoidable sunset of all that has been.

An Ou-topic City

Is Messina perhaps a Place? Is there still a faint trace of that *Geviert*, that Fourfold that allows human beings to call themselves "dwellers"? These questions seem hopeless or "out of place" because they are addressed to a city that has stubbornly made de-localization its first and only imperative. It is laughable, if not provocative, to invoke the divines and the mortals, and Heaven and Earth, in our current state of degradation. The de-culturation of the present makes us regret even the harsh ascesis of the desert. Messina is not simply a de-localized space, a pure desert or flat oceanic expanse, nor is it a blank slate on which we can simply write new rules. It is the deformity that leads back to formlessness, *chaos*, and anarchy. It is the absence of Principle and Limit. It is *Babel*—a city of total Confusion. Arriving at the city of Messina from the sea, visitors are confronted with a remarkable view, which has little to do with the usual image of a town. They find themselves faced with a messy jumble of cement, which looks like it has rained down on the land from no one knows where. They witness the devastation of a natural landscape, by now irremediably ruined, whose beauty can only be guessed at by straining the imagination. Rarely, I think, is such disharmony so apparent and so striking. At first glance, the city seems to be a chaotic disorder that is incapable

The Origin of Messina

71

of corresponding to the nature of a Place. When seen from the inside, though, Messina is truly hellish. It is not a city, but a river perpetually flooded by cars and trucks that move about at all hours. Their incessant and deafening noise overflows and invades every space. All that is left is desolation and degradation, rubbish and filth. The shameful slums and squalid neighborhoods that were once peripheral now crowd into the very heart of the city. The suburbs are overloaded with shopping centers and warehouses. Then there are the new settlements that vomit a concrete rain of terraced houses and megalithic residential complexes daily, adding new havoc to that which already exists.

How can we "dwell" here? How can we find a home in a city where everything seems to be subject to the logic of transit, passage, flowing, or building speculation? How can we *stay* in this furious current that drags humans and things along in its devastating course, leaving behind debris and rubbish that settle in large areas of devastation that are often forgotten?

Messina is as an *ou-topic* city, however ironic this definition may sound. We are accustomed to confusing utopia with *eu-to-pia*—that is to say, the idea of a happy space or a dream of an earthly paradise where we can finally attain a perfectly ordered and complete social and spatial organization. It is no coincidence that this dream soon turned into a nightmare in science fiction stories and in various attempts to put it into practice, as it is the concrete translation of a totalitarian immanentism that leaves no escape routes.

The idea of utopia derives from modernity and the celebration of scientific rationality. It became a favored literary trope because it related to the spirit of a time when the horror vacui, the fear of the void, was transformed into the exciting dream of a homogeneous and empty space. This fantasy space could be entirely controlled through the mathematization of reality and calculation, entirely subjected to the will to power of a *planning* that remains abstract because it stems from a soulless world that is deprived of any qualitative characteristic. On this void, on this *nothingness*, anything can be built, can be endlessly manipulated and transformed, including

72   GEOPHILOSOPHY OF THE MEDITERRANEAN

the natural environment and even human "nature" itself, as recent developments in biotechnology have clearly shown.

Ou-topia[8] refers, then, to that nihilistic de-localization that annihilates every qualitative difference. By transforming the Place into an amorphous space that is drastically reduced to a tabula rasa, this de-localization also deprives the Place of its intrinsic geohistorical character as well as its geosymbolic characteristics. Nietzsche speaks of a desert where the sand advances as far as the eye can see, in an unchanging space with no traceable or discernible limits. Schmitt speaks instead of an Ocean whose infinite expanse is an absolutely smooth surface that mocks every con-fine and every possible de-finition. These images are perhaps the most fitting way to describe the *nothing* around us and the loss of our ability to transform space into a habitable Place.

Messina's urban characteristics emerge out of this nothing, demonstrating that nothingness (that is, the absence of any plan) only permits the emergence of anarchic and chaotic spaces that are incapable of achieving a Form. Messina is a disconcerting mirror of this Formlessness, from which all its timid or reckless attempts to find its missing Place draw their inspiration. Perhaps we should simply conclude that Messina "has no place," having lost the memory of the Place it was once capable of being.

The Forgotten Origin

Er-örterung, at least in the way Heidegger uses the word, seems like the opposite of *Ent-ortung*. The latter refers to a nihilistic process of delocalization that strips away every root and erases every Where. *Er-örtern*, by contrast, means to "indicate the place," to search for the Place (*Ort*), and even to find it, not so much in a conservative attempt to revive the past but rather in the effort, entirely turned toward the future, to rediscover that Origin—never immediately attainable—from which alone a Place may emerge.

Going in search of the Place, of that Place that Messina has for a long time now ceased to be, means setting out toward

The Origin of Messina 73

its origin—that is, toward the origin of its *forma urbis*, its form of city. It is here that history and geomorphology meet, weaving an inextricable relationship that marked the destiny of the city from the very beginning. The meaning and the nature of this encounter have been lost, and this fact evidences the bewilderment and de-localization that now characterize its inhabitants, however unconsciously.

Where is the origin of Messina? There is undoubtedly only one answer to this question: as its oldest name, *Zankle*, reveals, the first urban settlement has an indissoluble geohistorical bond with the small, sickle-shaped strip of land (*zánklon*).[9] The city *begins* and takes form from the sickle, which, according to myth, Kronos wielded to castrate his father Uranus before throwing it, still covered in blood, into the sea. The story forever marked the city's destiny. The extraordinary geographical position of this tongue of land thrown into the middle of the Strait, with its rhythmic currents, has made Messina a Mediterranean city whose possible future depends on its ability to heed the call of its origin, that is, the close dialogue between land and sea from which it initially arose. This dialogue reached its apogee in the sixteenth and seventeenth centuries, when Jacopo Del Duca planned to tear down the medieval walls that defensively closed the urban space facing the Strait in order to open the city to direct contact with the sea. This plan testifies to the new awareness of the continuum that unites the sickle-shaped strip of land to the harbor quays. It will find an extraordinary and mature expression in the Palazzata, a sort of maritime theater that, in architect Filippo Juvarra's visionary project, was to extend as far as Cape Peloro. As Strabo, the Greek geographer and historian, correctly predicted, the Sickle (*Falce*) and Peloro now appear inseparably united,[10] in the shape of a terraqueous border that defines the city itself, from its point of origin to its far edge, where it is divided between *two* seas. Along this axis lies the city, which *begins* at the very tip of the Sickle and ends at the other tip, at Peloro, where in more ancient times the entire Island originated and took shape, cutting itself off from the continent. If Cape Peloro spreads into the sea like a prow, at the

74 GEOPHILOSOPHY OF THE MEDITERRANEAN

crossroads of the currents, the Sickle, by contrast, tries to encircle and sedate it, holding it in an embrace and offering the shelter of the port. It is only here, and not elsewhere, that we can perceive the original presence of Places, albeit in a scarred form. It is only here, in the counterpoint between the Sickle and Peloro, that Messina's *forma urbis* unfolds. It is only by recognizing the Sickle as its place of origin that Messina may still be able to find itself.

Here, the *Erörterung* can stop because the Place finally seems to reveal itself in its deep essence.

Between Sea and Land

Anyone who looks out onto the Strait of Messina immediately apprehends the complex geohistorical relevance of this site, which has no equal in the Mediterranean. One side, the *Lingua Phari*, with its curved arm and its concave shape, is a land that wedges itself into the sea of the Strait like a supple body slightly bent; its womb creates the harbor inlet, a space sheltered from winds and currents. On the other side, its back opens onto the sea of the Strait and exposes itself to the rhythmic meeting of the currents and the sirocco, the wind that comes from the south and the Sahara. One bank relates to the city reflected on the surface of a sea that is enclosed by the land, embraced, collected, and calmed within the shelter of the harbor womb. The other bank, by contrast, interacts with the continental edge *beyond* the sea and looks out at the water that separated it from the other land, constantly recalling this original fracture that made Sicily an island, *nésos*—something that sails, according to an Indo-European root.[11]

In addition to the relationship between these two seas, the Sickle also establishes a relationship between two lands: the sickle-shaped tongue of land that is called the *Lingua Phari* and the land onto which this strip is grafted, like an arm departing from a body to encircle the sea. The whole history of Messina has been shaped by this geomorphology, by this problematic relationship between arm and body. Closely joined to each other, so as to make

The Origin of Messina

the Sickle perceived as a peninsula, they were, however, more often violently separated and detached, to the point of making the Sickle an island. Such insularity is exemplified by the 1680 construction of the Citadel, which cut off the strip of land from the rest of the city, and even more by the architectural barrier created by the maritime station of the ferry boats, with its tangled tracks, as well as by the closure of large spaces occupied by the navy.

As a land-sea (*terramare*), this sickle-shaped land is an emblem of that incessant dialogue that is at the heart of the creation of Mediterranean cities. They do not lie at the edge of the Limitless, nor do they look out at the open sea of the ocean. The ocean is an immensurable space resistant to any nomos; it is a water desert on which it is impossible to draw boundaries or carve out shapes and figures, a smooth and uniform surface. It is a space of the beyond, a space of incessant crossing and absolute uprooting. On the contrary, nothing is more Mediterranean than the sea of Messina, which is *porthmós* and *póros* at the same time. It is a narrow sea arm surrounded by lands, a passage or flow, but is also held back and contained between earthen banks. Here, the juxtaposition and tension between land and sea is more pronounced than in other places of the Mediterranean. At its very beginnings, a tear and primordial caesura made Sicily an island, a floating *nésos* in the waters, facing a firmly anchored land, an *épeiros*, or terra firma. Scylla and Charybdis are the mythical references to the risk that is involved in this fracture, as the undying memory of an enduring contrast that simultaneously separates and unites seas and lands at the crossroads of the Mediterranean. Peloro is constantly faced with this *pólemos*, this strife; the two-faced Sickle constantly recalls it. It is only here that it is finally sedated, if only for an instant. As Heraclitus suggests, an invisible harmony opens up at the heart of the most lacerating discord. The unique morphology of the scythed strip of land is a surprising and eloquent proof of this harmony. It exposes itself to this contrast but quells it in the harbor; it stretches out into the sea but embraces it and holds it *still*. As Massimo Cacciari suggests, the *harbor* can only be the instant, *átopos* by definition, in which sea and land

76 GEOPHILOSOPHY OF THE MEDITERRANEAN

pass into each other. It is the Place of the greatest danger, where we *experience* the greatest danger.[12] While *ou-tópos* (unlocatable) is the space devoid of nomos, *a-tópos* is instead the in-between in which the Place itself opens up *between* sea and land, hovering in risk. Here, in the Sickle, one can see the cut that continually separates them but also, not with less evidence, the deep unity that connects them while keeping them in their absolute distinction. This is the visible place of the invisible harmony of the two. What else does the sheltered sea of the harbor attest, if not this precarious, unsustainable balance between sea and land, if not the war between the call of the Limitless, the Indefinite, and its incessant clash with the earthly border? As a place of maximum *insecuritas*, the harbor (both a point of arrival and departure) is the epitome of this insurmountable contrast, of a movement that constantly seeks a precarious balance between the earthly appeal to *stay* and the call of the sea to *go*. Nobody better than Homer's Ulysses has embodied this double tension in his journey between the ports of the Mediterranean. Nobody better than Dante's Ulysses has instead shown where the boundless call of the ocean leads us, insofar as it is a limitless sea, not surrounded by lands.[13]

The Sickle of the port of Messina has known similar Mediterranean navigators; its own inhabitants were among the most audacious travelers. But their journeys now seem to have decisively ended; once they had cast off the moorings, their departure was never followed by a return. The great emporium at the center of the Mediterranean, where merchandise, languages, cultures, and knowledge were exchanged, now seems only a distant memory, for the few who have any sense of history. Only things and people are now traveling between the two sides of the Strait, sliding fast, like on a highway. It seems that an invisible bridge over the Strait has already been built. Nothing is any longer able to quell this pendular movement that crosses the city, which has been reduced to a mere place of transit and passage. Messina is unable to rediscover the nomos that made it great, that equilibrium between land and sea that the Sickle, quietly and desperately, still demonstrates, despite everything, as an enduring hidden memory to those who are able to look beyond its evident degradation.

Anamnesis

Set apart from the city and its inhabitants, and from anyone else who would like to enjoy it, the sickle-shaped peninsula seems today an isolated no-man's-land, an island sailing adrift, completely forgotten, while its historical, landscape, and environmental memory appears in many ways irreparably ruined by human neglect. It is covered and concealed by an absolutely improper use of the spaces as well as by waste of all kinds that accentuates its desolation and degradation.

In the loss of its place of origin, Messina has forgotten its sea, just as it has forgotten its land. It is not easy to "inhabit" (a place) where the earth trembles and flattens everything we have painstakingly built, making a tabula rasa of the historical memory, where the earth is most *infirm* and precarious, constantly reminding us of the absolute vanity of our accomplishments as well as the radical finiteness of our lives. Finally, Messina seems to have surrendered to the precariousness and the transience of its destiny. Transit and passage have now become its devastating vocation, its self-defeating *cupio dissolvi*, its wish to be dissolved. It is as if the temporary earthquake has become a permanent state and a *norm*. Passages can only be crossed, though; they do not allow any possibility of abode. It is for this reason that Messina is no longer a Place. Being a citizen of Messina entails the impossibility of identifying oneself, of belonging to a definable space and time. Forgetful inhabitants wander about in the middle of this feverish movement that runs through the city, which trembles with unnoticed but incessant shocks.[14]

If the earth trembles, the sea, on the other hand, appears completely sedated: it is not a place of risk, or of exchange and confrontation with the other, but of mere connection between the

78   GEOPHILOSOPHY OF THE MEDITERRANEAN

two shores. Messina retains only an antiquarian and inattentive memory of the ancient beauty of its landscapes and monuments, now testified only by prints that are too ancient and distant in time to look at with due detachment. They are the last testimony of the relationship between the natural beauty of the site and the historic-artistic one, created by great architects such as Giovanni Angelo Montorsoli, Jacopo del Duca, Giovanni Antonio Ponzello, and Filippo Juvarra, who demonstrated in their works an astonishing geohistorical awareness. Almost no trace of all this is left. If the last earthquake razed the historical memory of the civic monuments to the ground, the subsequent reconstruction was no less devastating, as it was unable to interpret that geohistorical interweaving that alone would allow Messina to have and be a Place.

Almost a century has now passed since that terrible dawn of December 28, 1908, which erased identities and memories, swallowing the present together with the past as in an abyss. Ever since, Messina has been waiting for yet another beginning, waiting for the earthquake to end. And where to begin, if not from its own origin, from that thin curved strip of land, from that sickle of Kronos in which history and myth, sea and land prodigiously intersected at the very beginning, giving rise to Messina and making it a Place? Here, on the other hand, almost miraculously, there are still significant traces of a memory erased elsewhere: the extraordinary remains of the Citadel, Giovanni Montorsoli's lighthouse, and the ruins of the fort of San Salvatore, not to mention older remains that date back to the very first settlements.

A Place can only open up within a geohistorical awareness that the Place is called to exhibit. Without this memory, which always binds the history of the earth and the history of humans in a mysterious correspondence, no true dwelling is possible. Messina has a great historical past and a prodigious geographical and landscape location. Will it be able once again, as in the past, to find itself in its inevitable having become something else? It is evidently not a question of resurrecting the past but of *inheriting* it. The geohistorical memory, without which Messina is a *ou-topia*, a non-place, is not deposited as a series of data available in an archive that we can simply consult whenever we like. It does not look like a department store where old tools that are no longer usable lie more or less orderly or abandoned, according to a purely museum logic. Feeling heirs of the past means being able to make the past current once again, to correspond to it in new forms, to bear witness to it, while being aware of its being irretrievably past. Inheriting is not mere archiving, nor repetition; it is a legacy that we are called to assume in view of the future, so that there may be a future, since there can be no future without memory of the past.

The Sickle and, indeed, the entire city of Messina need this anamnesis to go back to their first beginning and, from there, to be able to start all over again. The city will be able to return to being a Place only if it is able to reappropriate its place of origin and, on that basis, go back to its original Form and thus rediscover what is proper to it. Will the Messina people be able to remember their origin? Will they be able to listen again to the unprecedented dialogue between land and sea that passed between the banks of the Strait? Will they be able to reunite the Sickle and Peloro in a new *forma urbis*? These are urgent questions and demands. So far, they seem to me to have fallen into the void. They have remained unheard, even mocked, by a completely oblivious citizenry, which has lost the sense of belonging and even seems indifferent to this need. We have become accustomed to *transit* and have totally lost the sense of *being*. Although it has now almost become invisible, that little sickle that rained from the sky into the heart of the Mediterranean reminds us of who we are, where we come from, where we might be headed to; it could perhaps offer us a Place for our dwelling, if it is still possible to dwell, in the harmonious accord of land and sea, under the vault of a very blue heaven. Will we once again be able to make it a habitable space?

Notes

Editor's Note

1. Gilles Deleuze and Félix Guattari, *Qu'est-ce que la philosophie?* (Paris: Minuit, 1991).

2. Luisa Bonesio and Caterina Resta, *Intervista sulla Geofilosofia*, ed. Riccardo Gardenal (Reggio Emilia: Diabasis, 2010), 9.

3. Massimo Cacciari, *Geofilosofia dell'Europa* (Milan: Adelphi, 1994) and *L'Arcipelago* (Milan: Adelphi, 1997).

4. Bonesio and Resta, *Intervista*, 10.

5. Caterina Resta, *La misura della differenza: Saggi su Heidegger* (Milan: Guerini, 1988).

6. Caterina Resta, *Il luogo e le vie: Geografie del pensiero in Martin Heidegger* (Milan: FrancoAngeli, 1996) and *La terra del mattino: Ethos, Logos e Physis nel pensiero di Martin Heidegger* (Milan: FrancoAngeli, 1998).

7. Caterina Resta, *Stato mondiale o* Nomos *della terra: Carl Schmitt tra universo e pluriverso* (Reggio Emilia: Diabasis, 2009).

8. Caterina Resta, *L'evento dell'altro: Etica e politica in Jacques Derrida* (Turin: Bollati Boringhieri, 2003), *L'Estraneo: Ostilità e ospitalità nel pensiero del Novecento* (Genoa: Il Melangolo, 2008), and *La passione dell'impossibile: Saggi su Jacques Derrida* (Genoa: Il Melangolo, 2016).

9. Caterina Resta, "Terramare," *Filosofia* 67 (2022): 13.

10. Resta, "Terramare," 13.

Preface

1. For years, this word has sought, in various ways, to try to think *together*, beyond the boundaries of disciplines, the various aspects that

82   NOTES TO CHAPTER ONE

shape the meaning of the relationship between human beings and the earth on which they live. The term suggests that thought must always be *rooted* in a land and that geographical elements are themselves charged with a value that goes beyond the merely natural to take on symbolic, historical, and philosophical values of extraordinary significance. There are many significant publications that explore geophilosophy, including Luisa Bonesio and Caterina Resta, *Intervista sulla Geofilosofia*, ed. Riccardo Gardenal (Reggio Emilia: Diabasis, 2010). Also of relevance are Massimo Cacciari, *Geofilosofia dell'Europa* (Milan: Adelphi, 1994) and *L'Arcipelago* (Milan: Adelphi, 1997); Franco Cassano, *Southern Thought and Other Essays on the Mediterranean*, ed. and trans. Norma Bouchard and Valerio Ferme (New York: Fordham University Press, 2012) and *Paeninsula: L'Italia da ritrovare* (Rome/Bari: Laterza, 1998).

Chapter One

1. As Heraclitus reminds us, "ἁρμονίη ἀφανὴς φανερῆς κρείσσων" (frag. 22B54, Diels-Kranz).

2. As there is now an extensive bibliography on the subject, we will limit ourselves here to citing Carlo Galli, *La guerra globale* (Rome/Bari: Laterza, 2002).

3. Schmitt's thinking on internationalization has been neglected for too long; it is, in my opinion, an important analysis that deals effectively with issues concerning the global era that emerged after the fall of the Berlin Wall. Of particular relevance are Carl Schmitt, *The Nomos of the Earth in the International Law of the Jus Publicum Europaeum*, trans. Gary L. Ulmen (New York: Telos Press, 2006) and, in particular for the present discussion, Schmitt, *Land and Sea*, trans. and with a foreword by Simona Draghici (Washington, DC: Plutarch Press, 1997). For a more in-depth discussion of issues relating to the end of the Eurocentric global order and the state-form it was based upon, as well as the development of a world State, see Caterina Resta, *Stato mondiale o Nomos della terra: Carl Schmitt tra universo e pluriverso* (Reggio Emilia: Diabasis, 2009). See also Carlo Galli's chapter "Schmitt e l'età globale" in Galli, *Lo sguardo di Giano: Saggi su Carl Schmitt* (Bologna: Il Mulino, 2008), 129–72; Carlo Galli, *Spazi politici: L'età moderna e l'età globale* (Bologna: Il Mulino, 2001).

4. Georg Wilhelm Friedrich Hegel, *Lectures on the Philosophy of World History*, trans. Hugh Barr Nisbet (Cambridge: Cambridge University Press, 1984), 196.

NOTES TO CHAPTER ONE

5. As Nietzsche remarks: "We stand in horror and awe before these prodigious remnants of what human beings used to be, and we have gloomy reflections about ancient Asia and its little protruding peninsula, Europe, that wants more than anything to upstage Asia and represent the 'progress of humanity.'" Friedrich Nietzsche, *Beyond Good and Evil: Prelude to a Philosophy of the Future*, trans. Adrian Del Caro, vol. 8 of *The Complete Works of Friedrich Nietzsche* (Stanford, CA: Stanford University Press, 2014), 53. The same image returns in Paul Valéry's "The Crisis of the Mind" (1919): "Will Europe become *what it is in reality*—that is, a little promontory on the continent of Asia? Or will it remain *what it seems*—that is, the elect portion of the terrestrial globe, the pearl of the sphere, the brain of a vast body?" Paul Valéry, *History and Politics*, trans. Denise Folliot and Jackson Mathews, vol. 10 of *The Collected Works of Paul Valéry*, ed. Jackson Mathews (London: Pantheon Books, 1963), 31. Again in "The European" (1922), Valéry ponders: "What, then, is Europe? It is a kind of cape of the old continent, a western appendix to Asia. It looks naturally toward the West." Valéry, *History and Politics*, 312. The first of these two quotations from Valéry features in a 1959 lecture by Martin Heidegger, "Hölderlin's Earth and Heaven," in *Elucidations of Hölderlin's Poetry*, trans. Keith Hoeller (Amherst, NY: Humanity Books, 2000), 201. Finally, there is the persistent work of deconstruction by Jacques Derrida, *The Other Heading: Reflections on Today's Europe*, trans. Pascale-Anne Brault and Michael B. Naas (Bloomington: Indiana University Press, 1992).

6. Hegel, *Lectures*, 170.

7. For further reading on the many names of the sea and the different meanings they convey, see the opening pages of Massimo Cacciari, *L'Arcipelago* (Milan: Adelphi, 1997).

8. See René Schérer, *Zeus hospitalier: Éloge de l'hospitalité: Essai philosophique* (Paris: Armand Colin, 1993).

9. The life and work of Louis Massignon is of significance here; see Louis Massignon, *L'hospitalité sacrée*, ed. Jacques Keryell (Paris: Nouvelle Cité, 1987) and *Trois prières d'Abraham* (Paris: Cerf, 1997).

10. This resonates throughout the Bible, from the Old to the New Testament: "[God] executes justice for the orphan and the widow, and befriends the alien, feeding and clothing him. So you too must befriend the alien, for you were once aliens yourselves in the land of Egypt" (Dt 10:18–19); "no stranger lodged in the street, but I opened my door to wayfarers" (Jb 31:32); "sharing your bread with the hungry, sheltering the oppressed and the homeless; clothing the naked when you see them,

84 NOTES TO CHAPTER ONE

and not turning your back on your own" (Is 58:7); "for I was hungry and you gave me food, I was thirsty and you gave me drink, a stranger and you welcomed me" (Mt 25:35). United States Conference of Catholic Bishops, *The New American Bible*, Nov. 11, 2002, https://www.vatican.va/archive/ENG0839/_INDEX.HTM. Many other passages could be cited. See Carmine Di Sante, *Lo straniero nella Bibbia: Saggio sull'ospitalità* (Troina: Città Aperta, 2002); Enzo Bianchi, *Ero straniero e mi avete ospitato* (Milan: Rizzoli, 2006).

11. Predrag Matvejević, *Mediterranean: A Cultural Landscape*, trans. Michael Henry Heim (Berkeley: University of California Press, 1999), 12.

12. On the loss of limit in the passage from an inland sea to oceanic size and for a deeper understanding of the complex of the issues raised here, see Cacciari's important analysis in Massimo Cacciari, *Geofilosofia dell'Europa* (Milan: Adelphi, 1994) and *L'Arcipelago*. Interesting ideas are also found in Franco Cassano, *Southern Thought and Other Essays on the Mediterranean*, ed. and trans. Norma Bouchard and Valerio Ferme (New York: Fordham University Press, 2012), where, among other things, we read:

> Europe, instead, becomes a world power when its gravitational center shifts from the Mediterranean to the Atlantic; when, as Carl Schmitt points out, the sea turns to its advantage the relationship with the land, accepting no boundaries and becoming ocean. The breach and eclipse of the Mediterranean coincide with the wane of moderation, and the rise of sea-based fundamentalism in complete opposition to land-based fundamentalism. The flowing of the sea beyond every boundary, its absolutization, marks the birth of modern economy, the unbridled freeing of technology, universal uprooting and total nomadism, and the disappearance of every return route, as man becomes a ship always at sea without moorings. It is the end of the coast, of the port, of those points where land and sea come into contact creating boundaries and thus knowing and limiting each other. (110–11)

For further reading on the difference between these two types of seas, see Francesca Saffioti, *Geofilosofia del mare: Tra oceano e Mediterraneo* (Reggio Emilia: Diabasis, 2007).

13. The contrast between Ulysses and Abraham is also emblematic of that between Greece and Judaism. For Levinas, it refers to the contrast

Notes to Chapter One

between a philosophy of self-return and of the Same, of which Hegel's *Phenomenology of Spirit* is certainly the most representative version, and a philosophy of "escaping" and of the precedence of the Other over the Same: "To the myth of Ulysses returning to Ithaca, we wish to oppose the story of Abraham who leaves his fatherland forever for a yet unknown land, and forbids his servant to even bring back his son to the point of departure" (348); Emmanuel Levinas, "The Trace of the Other," trans. Alphonso Lingis, in *Deconstruction in Context: Literature and Philosophy*, ed. Mark C. Taylor, 345–59 (Chicago: University of Chicago Press, 1986). For a comparison between these figures in relation to the Mediterranean, see Fabio Ciaramelli, "Tra Ulisse e Abramo: Il Mediterraneo come spazio immaginario," in *Il Mediterraneo: Fra tradizione e globalizzazione*, ed. Domenico Di Iasio, 37–58 (Lecce: Pensa Multimedia, 2007).

14. Cassano has effectively explored the Homeric figure of Ulysses and his Mediterranean characteristics in his *Southern Thought and Other Essays on the Mediterranean*.

15. The journey of Dante's Ulysses and its culmination in the "mad flight" has been extensively explored by Cacciari in *L'Arcipelago*, 63–71. See also Raffaele Giglio, *Il volo di Ulisse e di Dante: Altri studi sulla Commedia* (Naples: Loffredo, 1997) and its bibliography.

16. Of particular relevance here are Ovid, Virgil, Statius, Horace, Cicero, and Seneca.

17. Friedrich Nietzsche, *Unpublished Fragments from the Period of "Thus Spoke Zarathustra" (Summer 1882—Winter 1883/84)*, trans. Paul S. Loeb and David F. Tinsley (Stanford, CA: Stanford University Press, 2019), 25. Oswald Spengler's Columbus is in the same Nietzschean vein. He is an incarnation of the Faustian spirit and his "dark yearning for the boundless" (333). Like Copernicus, Columbus would have carried out a similar revolution of space, declaring "the victory of the infinite over the material limitedness of the tangibly present" (278), driven "by the adventured-craving for uncharted distances" (333), for unstoppable domination of ever larger spaces. Anticipating some of Schmitt's ideas, Spengler remarks that it was precisely from the era of great geographical discoveries that the Faustian civilization would have led the West to incorporate the whole world into itself:

> The discoveries of Columbus and Vasco da Gama extended the geographical horizon without limit, and the world sea came into the same relation with land as that of the universe of

space with earth. And then first the political tension within the Faustian world consciousness discharged itself. For the Greeks, Hellas was and remained the important part of the earth's surface, but with the discovery of America West Europe became a province in a gigantic whole. Thenceforward the history of the Western Culture has a planetary character. (334)

With Copernicus and Columbus, a boundless will to power began and came to define this civilization. A Faustian spirit was characterized by the desire for expansion and the desire for the unlimited:

The expansion of the Copernican world-picture into that aspect of stellar space that we possess to-day; the development of Columbus's discovery into a worldwide command of the earth's surface by the West, [. . .] the passion of our Civilization for swift transit, the conquest of the air, the exploration of the Polar regions and the climbing of almost impossible mountain-peaks we see, emerging everywhere the prime-symbol of the Faustian soul, Limitless Space. And those specially (in form, uniquely) Western creations of the soul-myth called "Will," "Force" and "Deed" must be regarded as derivatives of this prime-symbol. (337)

Oswald Spengler, *The Decline of the West*, vol. 1, *Form and Actuality*, trans. Charles F. Atkinson (New York: Knopf, 1996).

18. This is the title of aphorism 575, which concludes Friedrich Nietzsche, *Daybreak: Thoughts on the Prejudices of Morality*, ed. Maudemarie Clark and Brian Leiter, trans. R. J. Hollingdale (Cambridge: Cambridge University Press, 1997), 228.

19. Nietzsche, *Daybreak*, 228, 229.

20. Nietzsche, *Daybreak*, 229.

21. Nietzsche, *Daybreak*, 229, emphasis in original.

22. Nietzsche, *Daybreak*, 229.

23. Friedrich Nietzsche, *The Gay Science*, ed. Bernard Williams, trans. Josefine Nauckhoff (Cambridge: Cambridge University Press, 2001), 199.

24. Nietzsche, *Beyond Good and Evil*, 26.

25. Nietzsche, *Beyond Good and Evil*, 26.

26. Nietzsche, *Beyond Good and Evil*, 130.

Notes to Chapter Two

27. For more on this interpretation of Nietzsche, see Heidegger's extraordinary reading in Martin Heidegger, *Nietzsche*, ed. David Farrell Krell (San Francisco: Harper, 1995).

28. Nietzsche, *Gay Science*, 163, aphorism 289.

29. Nietzsche, *Daybreak*, 157.

30. Nietzsche, *Daybreak*, 157.

31. Nietzsche, *Daybreak*, 158.

32. Nietzsche, *Gay Science*, 119, aphorism 124. It is worth noting the strategic position of this aphorism. Clearly Nietzsche wished to highlight his announcement of God's death.

33. Carl Schmitt, "Dialogo sul nuovo spazio," in *Terra e mare: Una considerazione sulla storia del mondo*, trans. Angelo Bolaffi (Milan: Giuffrè, 1986), 99.

Chapter Two

1. See Edmund Husserl, "Philosophy and the Crisis of European Humanity," in *The Crisis of European Sciences and Transcendental Phenomenology: An Introduction to Phenomenological Philosophy*, trans. and with an introduction by David Carr (Evanston, IL: Northwestern University Press, 1970). For an analysis of the Husserlian perspective on Europe, see Renato Cristin, *La rinascita dell'Europa: Husserl, la civiltà europea e il destino dell'Occidente* (Rome: Donzelli, 2001). Although different from Husserl in his approach, De Giovanni also recognizes the essential link between Europe and philosophy (and, we should perhaps add, democracy) as genetically constitutive to the idea of Europe; see Biagio De Giovanni, "Le ragioni di Europa sono nella sua filosofia," in *Il Mediterraneo: Fra tradizione e globalizzazione*, ed. Domenico Di Iasio, 73–85 (Lecce: Pensa Multimedia, 2007). For a broader and more in-depth discussion, see Biagio De Giovanni, *L'ambigua potenza dell'Europa* (Naples: Guida, 2002) and *La filosofia e l'Europa moderna* (Bologna: Il Mulino, 2004).

2. See Serge Latouche, *The Westernization of the World: Significance, Scope and Limits of the Drive towards Global Uniformity*, trans. Rosemary Morris (Cambridge: Polity Press, 1996).

3. See Jacques Derrida, "Nel nome di Europa," trans. Caterina Resta, in *Geofilosofia*, ed. Marco Baldino, Luisa Bonesio, and Caterina Resta (Sondrio: Lyasis, 1996). This is a speech Derrida gave at Carrefour

88   Notes to Chapter Two

des littératures européennes de Strasbourg (November 7–10, 1992). The untitled transcript was published in *Géophilosophie de l'Europe: Penser l'Europe à ses frontières* (Paris: Editions de l'Aube, 1993).

4. See, in the present work, chapter 1, note 5.

5. Oswald Spengler, *The Decline of the West*, vol. 1, *Form and Actuality*, trans. Charles F. Atkinson (New York: Knopf, 1996).

6. These are the opening words of the first book of Friedrich Nietzsche, *The Will to Power*, ed. Walter Kaufmann, trans. Walter Kaufmann and R. J. Hollingdale (New York: Vintage Books, 1967), 7. This volume contains the controversial collection of posthumous fragments ordered and published by Peter Gast and Elisabeth Förster-Nietzsche in 1906.

7. See Carl Schmitt, *The Nomos of the Earth in the International Law of the Jus Publicum Europaeum*, trans. Gary L. Ulmen (New York: Telos Press, 2006). Conceived during the last years of the second world conflict in Nazi Germany and published in 1950, this important text is indispensable for understanding the history and "destiny" of Europe. On these issues, see also Caterina Resta, *Stato mondiale o Nomos della terra: Carl Schmitt tra universo e pluriverso* (Reggio Emilia: Diabasis, 2009).

8. In the impossibility of being able to give due space to this topic here, I refer to some texts that have focused more on the challenge that Auschwitz poses: Roberto De Pas, ed., *Pensare Auschwitz* (Milan: Thálassa De Paz, L. Gentili, Tranchida, 1995)—this volume is the translation of the special double issue of the journal *Pardès* 9–10 (1989), which collected the proceedings of the conference "Penser Auschwitz," held in Paris November 5–7, 1988; Giorgio Agamben, *Remnants of Auschwitz: The Witness and the Archive*, trans. Daniel Heller-Roazen (New York: Zone Books, 2000); Silvia Benso, *Pensare dopo Auschwitz: Etica filosofica e teodicea ebraica* (Naples: Esi, 1992); Philippe Lacoue-Labarthe and Jean-Luc Nancy, *Le mythe nazi* (Paris: L'Aube, 1991).

9. Julien Benda, Francesco Flora, Jean-R. de Salis, Jean Guéhenno, Denis de Rougemont, Georg Lukacs, Stephen Spender, Georges Bernanos, and Karl Jaspers, *L'esprit européen* (Paris: La Presse française et étrangère, 1947).

10. Both writings are contained in Martin Heidegger, *Off the Beaten Track*, ed. and trans. Julian Young and Kenneth Haynes (Cambridge: Cambridge University Press, 2002).

11. Martin Heidegger, *Introduction to Metaphysics*, trans. Gregory Fried and Richard Polt (New Haven, CT: Yale University Press, 2000), 40–54.

Notes to Chapter Two

12. See René Guénon, *The Reign of Quantity and the Signs of the Times*, trans. Walter E. C. James [Lord Northbourne] (London: Penguin, 1971), but important considerations in this regard are also found in René Guénon, *The Crisis of the Modern World*, 1927, trans. Marco Pallis, Arthur Osborne, and Richard C. Nicholson (Hillsdale, NY: Sophia Perennis, 2001).

13. Heidegger, *Metaphysics*, 47. On the permanence and ambiguities, within Heidegger's thought, of the term *spirit* and the meanings conveyed by it, see Jacques Derrida, *Of Spirit: Heidegger and the Question*, trans. Geoffrey Bennington and Rachel Bowlby (Chicago: University of Chicago Press, 1989).

14. Heidegger, *Metaphysics*, 40.

15. Heidegger, *Metaphysics*, 40.

16. Heidegger, *Metaphysics*, 40.

17. Martin Heidegger, *Contributions to Philosophy (Of the Event)*, trans. Richard Rojcewicz and Daniela Vallega-Neu (Bloomington: Indiana University Press, 2012), 314–15. This posthumous work, written between 1936 and 1938, during the years of the incredible rise of National Socialism, beyond a certain esotericism, perhaps provides not only one of the most acute interpretations of it but also its most radical counterpoint.

18. Heidegger, *Metaphysics*, 48.

19. Ernst Jünger, *The Worker: Dominion and Form*, ed. Laurence Paul Hemming, trans. Bogdan Costea and Laurence Paul Hemming (Evanston, IL: Northwestern University Press, 2017).

20. In this regard, see the much-misunderstood manifesto of Heideggerian antihumanism, written in 1946 in response to Jean Beaufret: Martin Heidegger, "Letter on Humanism," in *Pathmarks*, ed. William McNeill (Cambridge: Cambridge University Press, 1998). By deconstructing the fundamental stages of humanism, from the Greek beginning to Nietzsche, defining the human being as a rational animal, Heidegger does not intend to deny human beings at all but rather to give them back the essence that is their own but has been lost and betrayed by humanistic-subjectivistic interpretations. For a more in-depth analysis of these issues, see "Heidegger: Provocazione tecnica e umanità dell'umano" in Caterina Resta, *Nichilismo Tecnica Mondializzazione: Saggi su Schmitt, Jünger, Heidegger e Derrida*, 81–123 (Milan/Udine: Mimesis, 2013).

21. On the necessity of the "decline" for the coming of Europe, see the extraordinary theoretical work of Massimo Cacciari, *Geofilosofia dell'Europa* (Milan: Adelphi, 1994), which is an essential introduction to

90 NOTES TO CHAPTER TWO

Massimo Cacciari, *L'Arcipelago* (Milan: Adelphi, 1997). The reflections contained in these two precious volumes are, in my opinion, among the most penetrating analyses of the "European spirit," of its incurable *aporias* and its inevitable decline, as well as of the possibility of a "new beginning."

22. Martin Heidegger, "Overcoming Metaphysics," in *The End of Philosophy*, trans. Joan Stambaugh (Chicago: University of Chicago Press, 2003), 86.

23. Heidegger, *Off the Beaten Track*, 245.

24. Martin Heidegger, *What Is Called Thinking?*, trans. Fred D. Wieck and J. Glenn Gray (New York: Harper & Row, 1968), 70.

25. For a more in-depth analysis of this topic, see Caterina Resta, *La terra del mattino: Ethos, Logos e Physis nel pensiero di Martin Heidegger* (Milan: Angeli, 1998).

26. Martin Heidegger, "Hölderlin's Earth and Heaven," in *Elucidations of Hölderlin's Poetry*, trans. Keith Hoeller (New York: Humanity Books, 2000), 200.

27. Among the many texts that could be cited, in addition to those already mentioned, we limit ourselves to pointing out Julien Benda, *Discours à la nation europeenne* (Paris: Gallimard, 1992); Maria Zambrano, *La agonía de Europa* (Madrid: Trotta, 2000); Alberto Savinio, *Sorte dell'Europa 1943–1944* (Milan: Adelphi, 1977); José Ortega y Gasset, *Meditación de Europa y otros ensayos* (Madrid: Alianza Editorial, 2015); and Romano Guardini, *Europa: Compito e destino (1923–1962)*, ed. Silvano Zucal (Brescia: Morcelliana, 2004).

28. Jacques Derrida, *The Other Heading: Reflections on Today's Europe*, trans. Pascale-Anne Brault and Michael B. Naas (Bloomington: Indiana University Press, 1992), 77.

29. Derrida, *Other Heading*, 9.

30. For this aspect, see Caterina Resta, *L'Estraneo: Ostilità e ospitalità nel pensiero del Novecento* (Genoa: Il Melangolo, 2008).

31. See Jean-Luc Nancy, "À la frontière, figures et couleurs," in *Le désir d'Europe*, ed. Carrefour des littératures européennes, 41–50 (Paris: La Différence, 1992).

32. Schmitt and Jünger insisted, albeit with different accents, on the disturbing aspects of a world governed by technology. See Carl Schmitt, *L'unità del mondo e altri saggi* (Rome: Pellicani, 1994); Ernst Jünger, *Der Weltstaat: Organismus und Organisation* (Stuttgart: Klett, 1960). [Translator's note: *L'unità del mondo* is Schmitt's Italian anthology. Its essays were

NOTES TO CHAPTER THREE   91

previously published in *Lo stato*, an Italian journal of political science, law, and economy founded by Carlo Costamagna and Ettore Rosboch and published between 1930 and 1943.]

33. On the need to rethink the Mediterranean vocation of Europe and on the important geopolitical role of Italy as a "bridge" to the other side of the Mediterranean, see Franco Cassano, *Southern Thought and Other Essays on the Mediterranean*, ed. and trans. Norma Bouchard and Valerio Ferme (New York: Fordham University Press, 2012) and *Paeninsula: L'Italia da ritrovare* (Rome-Bari: Laterza, 1998). Further reading on the dynamics of globalization can be found in Pietro Barcellona, "Appunti sul Mediterraneo," in Di Iasio, *Mediterraneo*, 19–36.

34. Friedrich Nietzsche, *Unpublished Fragments (Spring 1885–Spring 1886)*, in vol. 16 of *The Complete Works of Friedrich Nietzsche*, based on the edition by Giorgio Colli and Mazzino Montinari, first organized in English by Ernst Behler, trans. Adrian Del Caro (Stanford, CA: Stanford University Press, 2020), 232, frag. 41[7].

Chapter Three

1. "So much has been said about this 'primary sea' converted into a maritime strait, and about its unity and division, and its homogeneity and disparity; we have known for a long time now that it is neither 'an independent reality' nor 'a constant,' but that the whole Mediterranean is composed of many sub-wholes that challenge or reject the unifying ideas." Predrag Matvejević, "The Mediterranean and Europe," *Quaderns de la Mediterrània* 10 (2008): 128.

2. As Montalbán correctly recalled, the imaginary representation of the barbarian, of the stranger, of the foreigner who arrives and destroys human and cultural relationships has weighed on the conscience of the men and women of the Mediterranean, creating a sensation of threatened space, which is not entirely realized. Since its very beginnings, the Mediterranean had been a place of passage, meeting, and conquest of those we conventionally call "barbarians." See Manuel Vázquez Montalbán, "La Méditerranée invertebrée," in *La Méditerranée espagnole*, Manuel Vázquez Montalbán and Eduardo González Calleja, 5–30 (Paris: Maisonneuve et Larose, 2000).

3. Marcella Delle Donne, *Un cimitero chiamato Mediterraneo: Per una storia del diritto d'asilo nell'Unione Europea* (Rome: Derive Approdi, 2004).

NOTES TO CHAPTER THREE

4. Predrag Matvejević, *Mediterranean: A Cultural Landscape*, trans. Michael Henry Heim (Berkeley: University of California Press, 1999), 23.

5. Matvejević, "The Mediterranean and Europe," 129–30.

6. "Mediterranean discourse has suffered from Mediterranean discursiveness: sun and sea, scent and color, sandy beaches and islands of fortune, [. . .] ports and ships and invitations au voyage, journeys and wrecks and tales thereof, oranges and olives and myrtle, palms and pines and cypresses, pomp and poverty, reality and illusion, life and dreams—such are the commonplaces plaguing the literature, all description and repetition. Mediterranean oratory has served democracy and demagogy, freedom and tyranny. [. . .] In every period and part of the region we find contradictions [. . .]: holy books of love and reconciliation along with crusades and jihads, the ecumenical spirit and fanatical ostracism, universality and autarchy." Matvejević, *Mediterranean: A Cultural Landscape*, 12.

7. Ferhat Horchani, "Tradizione e modernità: Le condizioni del dialogo fra le due sponde," in *Mediterraneo: Un dialogo fra le due sponde*, ed. Ferhat Horchani and Danilo Zolo (Rome: Jouvence, 2005), 159.

8. Horchani, "Tradizione e modernità," 159.

9. The influence of Ritter's historical geography has been extensively explored in Pietro Rossi, *Storia universale e geografia in Hegel* (Florence: Sansoni, 1975).

10. Georg Wilhelm Friedrich Hegel, *Lectures on the Philosophy of World History*, trans. Hugh Barr Nisbet (Cambridge: Cambridge University Press, 1984), 156 (italics in the original). Schmitt's geophilosophy derives from Hegel's and explores the relation between the land and the sea. It recognizes two contrasting ways of understanding the historical dynamics of the world as a whole: "World history is the history of the wars waged by maritime powers against land or continental powers and by land powers against sea or maritime powers." Carl Schmitt, *Land and Sea*, trans. and with a foreword by Simona Draghici (Washington, DC: Plutarch Press, 1997), 5.

11. Hegel, *Lectures*, 159.

12. "The *sea* in fact always gives rise to a particular way of life. Its indeterminate element gives us an impression of limitlessness and infinity, and when man feels himself part of this infinity, he is emboldened to step beyond his narrow existence. The sea itself is limitless, and it is not conducive to the peaceful and restricted life of cities as the inland regions are." Hegel, *Lectures*, 160.

13. See chapter 1 in the present volume.

Notes to Chapter Three

14. Hegel, *Lectures*, 161.

15. Georg Wilhelm Friedrich Hegel, *Elements of the Philosophy of Right*, ed. Allen W. Wood, trans. H. B. Nisbet (New York: Cambridge University Press, 1991), 268.

16. Hegel, *Lectures*, 161.

17. Hegel, *Lectures*, 171–72.

18. "*North Africa* lies on the Mediterranean Sea and extends westwards along the Atlantic; it is separated from southern Africa by the great desert—a waterless sea—and by the River Niger. The desert is a more effective division than the sea, and the character of the people who live immediately on the Niger reveals the difference between the two regions particularly clearly. [. . .] It includes the countries of Morocco, Fas (not Fez), Algeria, Tunis, and Tripoli. It could be said that this whole region does not really belong to Africa but forms a single unit with Spain, for both are part of one and the same basin. [. . .] This portion of Africa, like the Near East, is orientated towards Europe; it should and must be brought into the European sphere of influence." Hegel, *Lectures*, 173–74.

19. "America is therefore the country of the future, and its world-historical importance has yet to be revealed in the ages which lie ahead—perhaps in a conflict between North and South America. It is a land of desire for all those who are weary of the historical arsenal of old Europe." Hegel, *Lectures*, 170.

20. See Carl Schmitt, *The* Nomos *of the Earth in the International Law of the* Jus Publicum Europaeum, trans. Gary L. Ulmen (New York: Telos Press, 2006). In his work on geophilosophy, Schmitt engages in an intriguing comparison of the Old and New World. His analysis focuses on the European nomos that is based on the equilibrium between ground and sea—which we might call "Mediterranean"—and the validity of the Atlantic's American power, whose characteristics derive from the ocean and its *limitless* expanse. For more extensive scholarship on Schmitt's international outlook and in particular his geophilosophical thinking, see Caterina Resta, *Stato mondiale o* Nomos *della terra: Carl Schmitt tra universo e pluriverso* (Reggio Emilia: Diabasis, 2009).

21. Matvejević, *Mediterranean: A Cultural Landscape*, 12.

22. "Mediterranean man, instead, lives always between land and sea; he restrains one through the other." Franco Cassano, *Southern Thought and Other Essays on the Mediterranean*, ed. and trans. Norma Bouchard and Valerio Ferme (New York: Fordham University Press, 2012), 34. For more on Ulysses and the Mediterranean, see chapter 1 in the present work.

94   NOTES TO CHAPTER THREE

23. Baslez has extensively researched the Mediterranean routes that Paul took; see Marie-Françoise Baslez, *Saint Paul* (Paris: Fayard, 1991).

24. Danilo Zolo, "The Mediterranean Question and the 'Barcelona Process,'" *Jura Gentium* (2009), https://www.juragentium.org/topics/med/forum/en/zolo.htm. See also the preface to Horchani and Zolo, *Mediterraneo: Un dialogo*, 8 (this and other translations of Italian quotations are by Aisling Reid and Valentina Surace unless otherwise indicated):

> Europe, in its current subordination to the Atlantic, has forgotten its Mediterranean roots. It suffers a serious amputation which is the heart of its identity crisis and its lack of political autonomy, as well as its impotence on the international stage. Europe is forced to think of itself as "Old Europe," i.e., as an outdated phase of the historical development that led to the affirmation of Western civilization. From this perspective, Europe is identical to the United States, except for its political and military backwardness, which makes it a parasite on the American superpower. [. . .] A Europe that rediscovers its Mediterranean roots could emerge [. . .] as a space for mediation and neutralization of opposing fundamentalisms.

25. Fernand Braudel, "The Mediterranean: Land, Sea, History," *The Courier* 38, no. 12 (1985): 4, https://unesdoc.unesco.org/ark:/48223/pf0000067900.

26. Fernand Braudel, "Preface to the First Edition," in *The Mediterranean and the Mediterranean World in the Age of Philip II*, by Fernand Braudel, vol. 1, trans. Siân Reynolds (New York: Harper & Row, 1972), 17.

27. Fernand Braudel, *La Méditerranée, l'espace et l'histoire* (Paris: Flammarion, 1985), 158.

28. Matvejević, *Mediterranean: A Cultural Landscape*, 10.

29. Braudel, *La Méditerranée, l'espace et l'histoire*, 172.

30. "The image offered by the Mediterranean is far from reassuring. [. . .] It is not really possible to consider this sea as one 'whole' without bearing in mind the fractures that divide it and the conflicts that tear it apart [. . .] We have witnessed the cruel failure of the implementation of coexistence in multiethnic or multinational territories, in which diverse cultures and distinct religions cross and mix." Matvejević, "The Mediterranean and Europe," 127–28.

Notes to Chapter Three

31. Braudel, *La Méditerranée, l'espace et l'histoire*, 173.

32. Matvejević, "The Mediterranean and Europe," 128.

33. "However, despite the splits and the conflicts that take place or that are suffered in this part of the world, there are common or accessible ways of being and ways of living." Matvejević, "The Mediterranean and Europe," 129.

34. As Derrida has remarked: "*what is proper to a culture is to not be identical to itself.*" Jacques Derrida, *The Other Heading: Reflections on Today's Europe*, trans. Pascale-Anne Brault and Michael Naas (Bloomington: Indiana University Press, 1992), 9. For a more extensive analysis on the issue, see Caterina Resta, "Un'esposizione vulnerabile," *Φάσις: European Journal of Philosophy: Ex-position* 0 (2012): 141–61.

35. Braudel, "The Mediterranean: Land, Sea, History," 5.

36. Cassano has extensively researched the pluriversal nature of this geohistoircal issue: "The Mediterranean that emerges is not a monolithic identity, but a multiverse that trains the mind to grasp the complexities of the world: hybridity, crossroads, and identities that do not love purity and cleanliness, but have been mixed for a long time." Cassano, *Southern Thought*, 137. Ciaramelli also insists on the paradigmatic character of the Mediterranean as a "unity of the multiple"; see Fabio Ciaramelli, "Tra Ulisse e Abramo: Il Mediterraneo come spazio immaginario," in *Il Mediterraneo: Fra tradizione e globalizzazione*, ed. Domenico Di Iasio (Lecce: Pensa Multimedia 2007), 37–58. According to Ciaramelli,

> looking more closely at the situation from an historical-anthropological point of view, the Mediterranean space constitutes a protean unity; it is a stratified and complex reality that cannot be read as the bearer of a monolithic cultural identity. Far from constituting the expression of a stable unitary identity or of a determined geographical, historical or cultural essence, stiffened in its codified configurations, the Mediterranean area appears above all to be characterized by its nature as an unstable frontier between different worlds, on some points even opposites, and for this very reason mutually attracted. (40)

37. We might be reminded of the Norman kingdom of Roger II of Hauteville or the court of Frederick II of Swabia, in Palermo, open to the four cultures: Greek, Latin, Jewish, and Muslim.

96 NOTES TO CHAPTER THREE

38. See Massimo Cacciari, "Nomi di luogo: confine," *aut aut* 299–300 (2000); the chapter entitled "Thinking the Frontier" in Cassano, *Southern Thought*, 41–51.

39. Ciaramelli, "Tra Ulisse e Abramo," 57.

40. Cassano, *Southern Thought*, 37. Ciaramelli similarly addresses the issue:

> In the very beginning, *borders* were places of division and opposition, places of men who stand in front of each other, each of whom watches over the other. [. . .] At the *border*, at the *limit* every one of us *ends* and becomes defined. We acquire form and accept our being limited by something else which is obviously and also limited by us. The end determines and the boundary de-fines. [. . .] The border therefore does not unite *and* separate, but unites *as* it separates. ("Tra Ulisse e Abramo," 54–55)

41. Horchani and Zolo, preface to *Mediterraneo: Un dialogo*, 7.

42. Horchani and Zolo, 7.

43. For further reading on this issue, see the work by Franco Cassano and Danilo Zolo in *L'alternativa mediterranea*, ed. Cassano and Zolo (Milan: Feltrinelli, 2007).

44. As Zolo remarks, "unity" does not entail cultural uniformity or monotheism. On the contrary, it entails the full inclusion within the Mediterranean cultural "pluriverse" of the Arab Islamic civilization, which stretches from the Maghreb to the Mashreq, from Morocco to Egypt to Syria, as "the Mediterranean has always been an irreducible 'pluriverse' of peoples, languages, artistic expressions and religions that no Empire, not even the Roman empire, ever managed to conquer and control tightly" ("Mediterranean Question"). On the need for dialogue with the Arab Islamic world, see Horchani and Zolo, *Mediterraneo: Un dialogo*.

45. As Cassano has demonstrated, the Mediterranean invites us to think of another universalism beyond any of the abstractness that is often disrespectful of differences: "*It is neither a universal truth defined by the strongest nor a relativistic closure of cultures within themselves, but the complex construction of a polyphonic universal*" (*Southern Thought*, 149; emphasis in the original). This kind of "universalism is not dogmatic and a priori, but syncretic and a posteriori; it is a universalism that is always imperfect and lives on translations" (152).

Notes to Chapter Four

46. Cassano, *Southern Thought*, 142.

47. The Greek term *nesos* (island) derives from the verb *necho*: to swim, to float on water, to navigate.

48. Cassano explores the idea of "translation" in *Southern Thought*, 50–51. Bauman contrasts the paradigm of translation with that of identity multiculturalism; see Zygmunt Bauman, *In Search of Politics* (Cambridge: Polity Press, 2006), 197–202. For thinking about translation in the sense explored here, see Jacques Derrida, *Monolingualism of the Other; or, The Prosthesis of Origin*, trans. Patrick Mensah (Stanford, CA: Stanford University Press, 1998). For a more in-depth analysis of the topic of translation, including Benjamin, Heidegger, and Derrida, see Caterina Resta, "Necessità della traduzione," in *La misura della differenza: Saggi su Heidegger*, 111–95 (Milan: Guerini, 1988).

49. See Francesco Gioia, *Pellegrini e forestieri nel mondo antico* (Milan: Mondadori, 1998).

50. See Horchani and Zolo, preface to *Mediterraneo: Un dialogo*, 9.

51. Zolo, "Mediterranean Question."

Chapter Four

1. On the cartographic imagination, see Franco Farinelli, *L'invenzione della terra* (Palermo: Sellerio, 2007) and *Blinding Polyphemus: Geography and the Models of the World*, trans. Christina Chalmers (London: Seagull Books, 2021).

2. For the use of this term, see Luisa Bonesio and Caterina Resta, *Intervista sulla Geofilosofia*, ed. Riccardo Gardenal (Reggio Emilia: Diabasis, 2010).

3. On this extraordinary man and his reign, see Denis Mack Smith, *A History of Sicily*, 2 vols. (New York: Dorset, 1988); Carlo Ruta, *I normanni in Sicilia* (Palermo: Promolibri, 2007); Hubert Houben, *Roger II of Sicily: A Ruler between East and West*, trans. Graham A. Loud and Diane Milburn (Cambridge: Cambridge University Press, 2002).

4. Idrisi, "The Book of Roger by Abû 'Abdallâh al-Idrîsî," in *Roger II and the Creation of the Kingdom of Sicily*, trans. Graham A. Loud, 355–63 (Manchester: Manchester University Press, 2012).

5. See Fernand Braudel, *La Méditerranée, l'espace et l'histoire* (Paris: Flammarion, 1985); Massimo Cacciari, *L'Arcipelago* (Milan: Adelphi, 1997); Franco Cassano, *Southern Thought and Other Essays on the Mediterranean*,

98 NOTES TO CHAPTER FIVE

ed. and trans. Norma Bouchard and Valerio Ferme (New York: Fordham University Press, 2012) and *Paeninsula: L'Italia da ritrovare* (Rome-Bari: Laterza, 1998); Predrag Matvejević, *Mediterranean: A Cultural Landscape*, trans. Michael Henry Heim (Berkeley: University of California Press, 1999); Ferhart Horchani and Danilo Zolo, eds., *Mediterraneo: Un dialogo fra le due sponde* (Rome: Jouvence, 2005).

6. Franco Cassano and Danilo Zolo, *L'alternativa mediterranea* (Milan: Feltrinelli, 2007).

Chapter Five

1. Martin Heidegger, "Language in the Poem: A Discussion on Georg Trakl's Poetic Work," in *On the Way to Language*, trans. Peter D. Hertz (New York: Harper & Row, 1971), 159–60. Here, we have adapted an English translation of the original German text. See Martin Heidegger, "Die Sprache im Gedicht: Eine Erörterung von Georg Trakls Gedicht," in *Unterwegs zur Sprache*, vol. 12 of *Gesamtausgabe* (Frankfurt am Main: Vittorio Klostermann, 1985), 53. Moreover, we have preferred to translate *Ort* as *place* instead of *site* or *location*, which are the terms that have been used by Heidegger's translators.

2. For the symbolism of the center, see René Guénon, *Symbols of Sacred Science*, trans. Henry D. Fohr, ed. Samuel D. Fohr (Hillsdale, NY: Sophia Perennis, 2004); Mircea Eliade, *Images and Symbols: Studies in Religious Symbolism*, trans. Philip Mairet (Princeton, NJ: Princeton University Press, 1991).

3. See Martin Heidegger, "Building Dwelling Thinking," in *Poetry, Language, Thought*, trans. Albert Hofstadter (New York: Harper Colophon Books, 1971).

4. For this meaning of *place*, as clearly differentiated from that of merely geometric space, see Luisa Bonesio and Caterina Resta, *Intervista sulla Geofilosofia*, ed. Riccardo Gardenal (Reggio Emilia: Diabasis, 2010). All of Bonesio's important research on the landscape is inspired by this decisive distinction; see Luisa Bonesio, *Geofilosofia del paesaggio* (Milan: Mimesis, 1997); *Oltre il paesaggio: I luoghi tra estetica e geofilosofia* (Casalecchio: Arianna, 2002); and *Paesaggio, identità e comunità tra locale e globale* (Reggio Emilia: Diabasis, 2007); as well as Luisa Bonesio, ed., *Orizzonti della geofilosofia: Terra e luoghi nell'epoca della mondializzazione* (Casalecchio: Arianna, 2000).

NOTES TO CHAPTER FIVE

5. Heidegger, "Building Dwelling Thinking," 158.

6. See Marc Augé, *Non-Places: An Introduction to an Anthropology of Supermodernity*, trans. John Howe (London: Verso, 1995).

7. For an in-depth analysis of these crucial questions, see Caterina Resta, *Il luogo e le vie: Geografie del pensiero in Martin Heidegger* (Milan: Angeli, 1996); *Stato mondiale o Nomos della terra: Carl Schmitt tra universo e pluriverso* (Reggio Emilia: Diabasis, 2009); and, with Luisa Bonesio, *Passaggi al bosco: Ernst Jünger nell'era dei Titani* (Milan: Mimesis, 2000).

8. It is in this sense that Carl Schmitt closely combines utopia and nihilism in the (entirely modern) perspective of an inexorable *Entortung*; see Carl Schmitt, *The Nomos of the Earth in the International Law of the Jus Publicum Europaeum*, trans. Gary L. Ulmen (New York: Telos Press, 2006), 66 and 178. See also Massimo Cacciari, "Di naufragi e utopie," in *L'Arcipelago*, 63–91 (Milan: Adelphi, 1997), who speaks of it in this same sense.

9. See Anna Maria Prestianni Giallombardo, "La falce-porto di Zankle-Messana: Dall'alto arcaismo alla tarda antichità," in *La penisola di San Raineri: Diaspora dell'origine*, ed. Nicola Aricò, special issue, *DRP* 4 (2002): 129–54. The various contributions to this monographic issue of the magazine are entirely devoted to the sickle of the port of Messina. They have also been important sources for my reflections in this essay.

10. For the "closed dialogue between Zankle and Peloro," see Nicola Aricò, *Illimite Peloro: Interpretazioni del confine terracqueo: Montorsoli, Del Duca, Ponzello, Juvarra, D'Arrigo* (Messina: Mesogea, 1999), 65. My reflections owe much to this important text. The close relationship between the Sickle and Peloro is also underlined by Anna Maria Prestianni Giallombardo, "Il Peloro nell'antichità: Miti Scienze Storia," in *Messina e Reggio nell'antichità: Storia, società, cultura*, ed. Bruno Gentili and Antonino Pinzone (Soveria Mannelli: Di.Sc.A.M./Rubbettino, 2002).

11. See Predrag Matvejević, *Mediterranean: A Cultural Landscape*, trans. Michael Henry Heim (Berkeley: University of California Press, 1999), 162: "Etymologists associate the Greek word for island, *nêsos*, with the Indo-European root meaning 'floating.'"

12. See Massimo Cacciari, preface to Aricò, *Illimite Peloro*, 5.

13. On Ulysses in Homer and Dante, see Cacciari, *L'Arcipelago*.

14. An insightful and brief description of the political-institutional and civil decline of the city is found in Massimo La Torre, *Messina come metafora e luogo idealtipico della politica* (Soveria Mannelli: Rubbettino, 2000). In his perceptive analysis, La Torre highlights how the 1908

earthquake, in particular, with the consequent annihilation of the city bourgeoisie and the disappearance of civil society, marked a "biopolitical" turning point: citizens appear increasingly concerned about their own "private" and "natural" survival, willing to ask for "favours" to satisfy their *elementary* needs instead of claiming rights, in the progressive disappearance of any "public" space. It follows as a consequence that human beings (the Messinesi) feel free only in their animal functions, such as eating, drinking, procreating, and, at most, living in a house and dressing themselves, whereas they feel nothing more than a beast in their human functions. What is animal becomes human, and what is human becomes animal. The entire first part of the book is dedicated to the importance of reawakening the historical memory of the city in order to be able to draw its *origin* from the sickle-shaped peninsula of San Raineri.

Index

Abraham, 3, 4, 83n9, 84n13
America, 2, 10, 11, 17, 19, 20, 28, 41, 42, 86n17, 93n19
Al-Idrisi, 55, 57, 58, 59, 60, 61, 62, 63, 64, 97n4

Bonesio, Luisa, xix, 82n1, 87n3, 97n2, 98n4, 99n7
border, 2, 3, 4, 5, 10, 11, 15, 17, 24, 26, 27, 30, 31, 32, 33, 36, 41, 46, 47, 53, 60, 63, 73, 76, 96n40
boundary, 9, 38, 42, 53, 75, 81n1, 84n12
boundless, 2, 7, 76, 85–86n17
Braudel, Fernand, 43, 44, 45, 46, 94n25, 94n26, 94n27, 94n29, 95n31, 95n35, 97n5

Cacciari, Massimo, 75, 82n1, 83n7, 84n12, 85n15, 89–90n21, 96n38, 97n5, 99n8, 99n12, 99n13
Cassano, Franco, 48, 82n1, 84n12, 85n14, 91n33, 93n22, 95n36, 96n38, 96n40, 96n43, 96n45, 97n46, 97n48, 97n5, 98n6

Columbus, Christopher, 3, 6, 7, 8, 10, 43, 85–86n17

de-localization, 69, 70, 72, 73
Derrida, Jacques, 14, 17, 25, 83n5, 87n2, 89n13, 89n20, 90n28, 90n29, 95n34, 97n48
dialogue, 1, 3, 11, 12, 14, 31, 33, 45, 48, 49, 50, 63, 73, 75, 79, 96n44, 99n10
dwelling, xx, 6, 68, 78, 79, 98n3, 99n5, 101

extraneous, 15; extraneousness, 49, 50. See also foreign

foreign, xviii, 30, 31, 45; foreigner, 3, 25, 91n2. See also extraneous

Hegel, Georg Wilhelm Friedrich, 2, 13, 38, 39, 40, 41, 42, 82n4, 83n6, 85n13, 92n9, 92nn10–12, 93nn14–19
Heidegger, Martin, 13, 14, 17, 18, 20, 21, 22, 23, 62, 68, 69, 72, 83n5, 87n27, 88n10, 88n11, 89n13–18, 89n20, 90n22–26, 97n48, 98n1, 98n3, 99n5, 99n7

identity, xix, xx, 11, 14, 15, 24,
25, 27, 28, 29, 30, 31, 33,
37, 46, 47, 53, 63, 78, 94n23,
95n36, 97n48, 98n4
island, xvii, xviii, xix, xx, 2, 3,
4, 6, 10, 11, 32, 42, 44, 47,
49, 53, 54, 60, 73, 74, 75, 77,
92n6, 97n47, 99n11

Jünger, Ernst, 14, 18, 20, 21,
69, 89n19, 89n20, 90n32,
99n7

large space 48; large hemispheres,
19. *See also* wide area
Levinas, Emmanuel, 4, 14,
84–85n13

Matvejević, Predrag, 3, 36, 44,
45, 84n11, 91n1, 92nn4–6,
93n21, 94n28, 94n30, 95n32,
95n33, 98n5, 99n11
Messina, xvii, xviii, xx, 67,
70–79, 71, 72, 73, 74, 75,
76, 77, 78, 79, 99n9, 99n10,
99n14; Strait (of Messina), 54,
73, 74, 76, 79

New World, 3, 8, 32, 34, 43, 48,
64, 93n20
Nietzsche, Friedrich, 6, 7, 8, 9,
10, 17, 18, 21, 22, 29, 33, 38,
69, 72, 83n5, 85n17, 86nn18–
32, 88n6, 89n20, 91n34
nomos, 9, 10, 12, 18, 33, 50, 69,
75, 76, 82n3, 88n7, 93n20,
99n7–8

ocean, 2, 3, 4, 5, 6, 7, 8, 9, 10,
11, 32, 33, 35, 39, 40, 41,

42, 43, 70, 72, 75, 76, 84n12,
93n20; oceanic, 2, 3, 5, 9, 11,
19, 41, 42, 43, 62, 70, 84n12
Odysseus, 3, 4. *See also* Ulysses

pluriverse, 12, 33, 47, 48, 49, 50,
64, 96n44; pluriversal, 12, 33,
95n36; pluriverso, 82n3, 88n7,
93n20, 99n7

Schmitt, Carl, 2, 10, 17, 18, 20,
39, 41, 69, 72, 82n3, 84n12,
87n33, 88n7, 89n20, 90n32,
92n10, 93n20, 99n7, 99n8
Sicily, xvii, xix, xx, 4, 44, 53, 55,
56, 57, 60, 61, 62, 63, 65, 74,
75, 97n3, 97n4
Spengler, Oswald, 18, 86n17

translation, 12, 26, 27, 33, 49, 50,
64, 71, 96n45, 97n48

Ulysses, 3, 4, 5, 6, 7, 8, 11, 41,
76, 84–85n13, 85n14, 85n15,
93n22, 99n13
uprooting, xvii, xix, xx, 23, 69,
72, 84; strips away every root,
75

Valéry, Paul, 17, 83n5

war, xiv, 1, 2, 3, 11, 18, 19, 20,
21, 24, 29, 30, 37, 45, 46, 47,
48, 54, 76, 92n10
wide area, 48; wide space, 9, 64
See also large space

Zolo, Danilo, 43, 92n7, 94n24,
96n41, 96n42, 96n43, 96n44,
97n50, 97n51, 98n5, 98n6

About the Author

Caterina Resta teaches courses on twentieth-century philosophy at the University of Messina, Italy. She has worked extensively on Heidegger, Jünger, and Schmitt as well as on issues of otherness and difference, including gender, engaging with the thought of Derrida, Nancy, and Levinas. For a number of years, she has devoted herself to cultivating an innovative geophilosophical perspective as a means of rethinking the human "dwelling" on the earth in the current era of globalization. Her publications include *L'Estraneo: Ostilità e ospitalità nel pensiero del Novecento* (2008); *Stato mondiale o Nomos della terra: Carl Schmitt tra universo e pluriverso* (2009); *Intervista sulla Geofilosofia* (with Luisa Bonesio, 2010); and *La passione dell'impossibile: Saggi su Jacques Derrida* (2016). Some of her work that has appeared in English includes "Walled Borders: Beyond the Barriers of Immunity of the Nation-States," in *Debating and Defining Borders: Philosophical and Theoretical Perspectives,* edited by Anthony Cooper and Søren Tinning (2020); "The Age of the Totalitarian Domination of Technology," in *Heidegger and Contemporary Philosophy: Technology, Living, Society & Science,* edited by Carmine Di Martino (2021); "Immunitary Politics," in *Contemporary Italian Women Philosophers: Stretching the Art of Thinking,* edited by Silvia Benso and Elvira Roncalli (2021); and "Vulnerable Existences," in *Rethinking Life: Italian Philosophy in Precarious Times,* edited by Silvia Benso (2022).